Missouri

MISSOURI BY ROAD

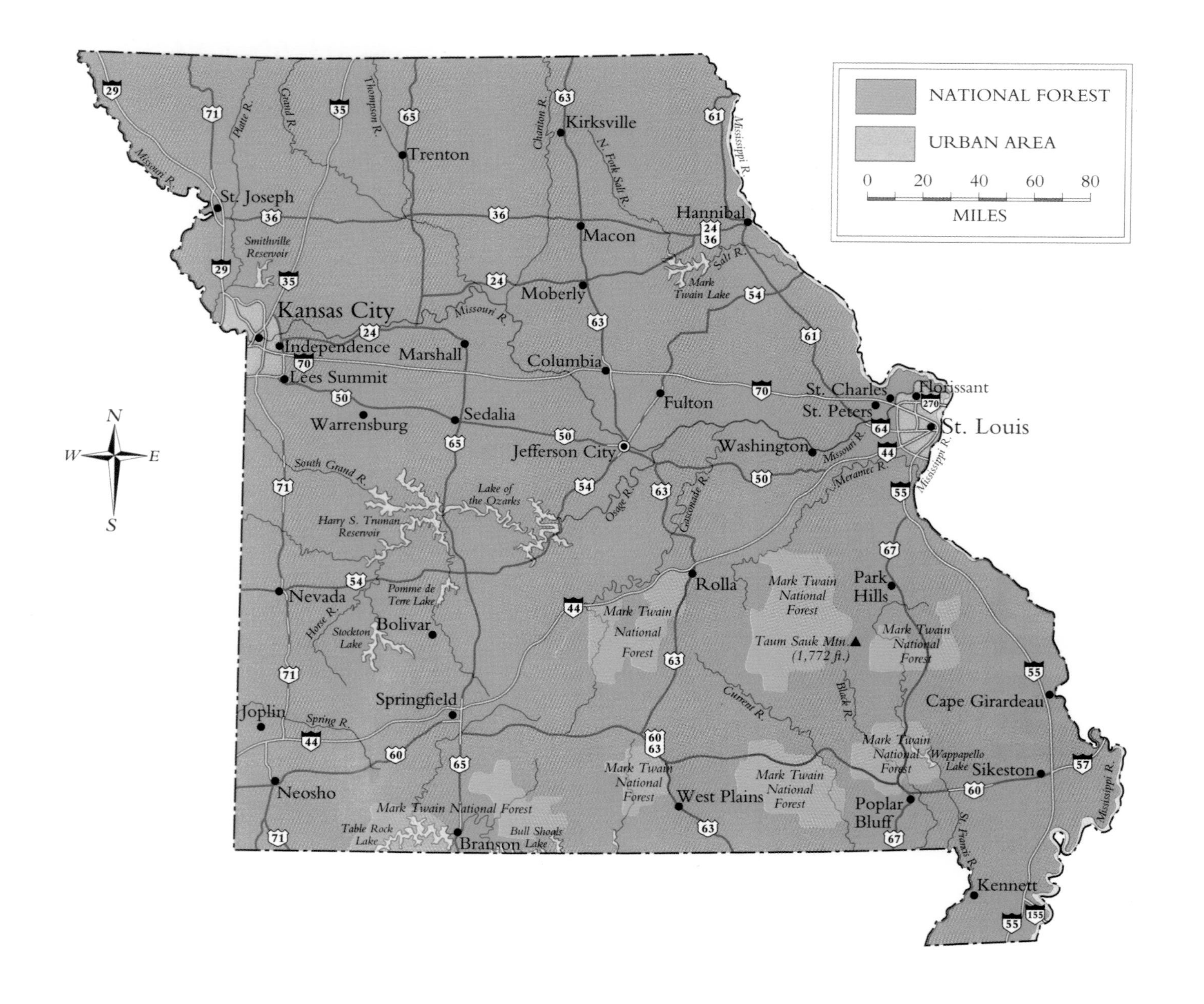

Celebrate the States

MISSOURI

Michelle Bennett and Joyce Hart

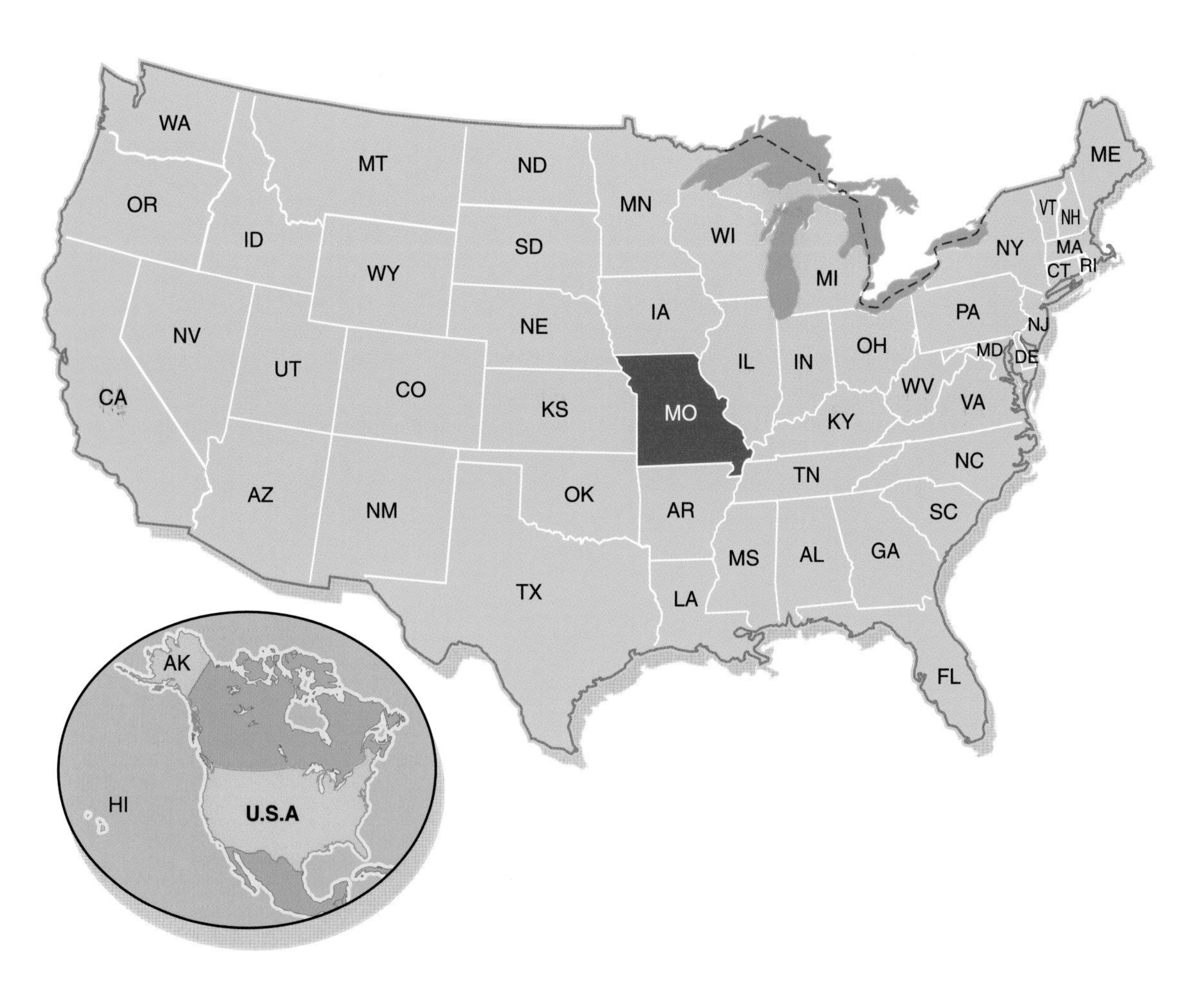

Marshall Cavendish Benchmark
New York

Published by Marshall Cavendish Benchmark
An imprint of Marshall Cavendish Corporation

Website: www.marshallcavendish.us

Other Marshall Cavendish Offices:
Marshall Cavendish Ltd. 5th Floor, 32-38 Saffron Hill, London EC1N 8 FH, UK • Marshall Cavendish International (Asia) Private Limited, 1 New Industrial Road, Singapore 536196 • Marshall Cavendish International (Thailand) Co Ltd. 253 Asoke, 12th Flr, Sukhumvit 21 Road, Klongtoey Nua, Wattana, Bangkok 10110, Thailand • Marshall Cavendish (Malaysia) Sdn Bhd, Times Subang, Lot 46, Subang Hi-Tech Industrial Park, Batu Tiga, 40000 Shah Alam, Selangor Darul Ehsan, Malaysia

Library of Congress Cataloging-in-Publication Data
Bennett, Michelle.
Missouri / by Michelle Bennett and Joyce Hart.—2nd ed.
p. cm. — (Celebrate the states)
Summary: "Provides comprehensive information on the geography, history, wildlife, governmental structure, economy, cultural diversity, peoples, religion, and landmarks of Missouri"—Provided by publisher.
Includes bibliographical references and index.
ISBN 978-0-7614-4727-6
1. Missouri—Juvenile literature. I. Hart, Joyce, 1954– II. Title.

F466.3.B46 2011
977.8—dc22
2009005754

Editor: Christine Florie
Co-Editor: Denise Pangia
Publisher: Michelle Bisson
Art Director: Anahid Hamparian
Series Designer: Adam Mietlowski

Photo research and layout by Marshall Cavendish International (Asia) Private Limited—
Thomas Khoo, Benson Tan and Gu Jing

Cover Photo by Photolibrary

The photographs in this book are used by permission and through the courtesy of; *Associated Press*: 68; *Bes Stock*: 123; *Corbis*: 13, 43, 47, 64, 81, 86, 88, 96, 100, 114, 117, 118, 120, 121, 122, 124, 125, 126, 127, 132, 133, 136; *Gettyimages*: 76, 119, 128, 129; *Lonely Planet*: 102; *National Geographic Image Collection*: 30; *North Wind Picture Archives*: 41; *Photolibrary*: back cover, 8, 12, 16, 19, 21, 22, 23, 26, 31, 33, 35, 50, 59, 73, 74, 83, 93, 98, 105, 108, 113, 130, 131; *Photolibrary/Alamy*: 11, 18, 40, 52, 60, 61, 66, 90, 92, 97, 101, 115, 134, 135; Randall Hyman: 55; *Southeastern Archeological Center, National Park Service*: Martin Pate, Newnan GA, 29.

Printed in Malaysia
1 3 5 6 4 2

Contents

Missouri Is . . .

Missouri is right at the center of America.

"A Missouriian gets used to Southerners thinking him a Yankee, a Northerner considering him a cracker, a Westerner sneering at his effete Easternness, and the Easterner taking him for a cowhand."

—William Least Heat-Moon, Missouri writer

"I have learned that we must always work to strengthen the civic fabric that binds us together as one people. Tomorrow's Missouri and America depend upon how we surmount whatever challenges come our way."

—U.S. senator Kit Bond

Missourians are a bit old-fashioned . . .

"Missouri, though some Missourians may not like to hear it, is a rural-minded country. The flavor of a premachine-age past hangs in its drawling speech. In the skepticism of its people there is a good deal of the old doubting backwoods farmer who isn't going to be dragged into newfangled situations without long consideration. Missouri is a state which does not rush wildly to decision."

—Thomas Hart Benton, artist

. . . and sometimes leery of strangers.

"Not much traffic comes through some of those places. If an outsider comes over the hill, wearing something different or doing something curious, they are not hesitant to look you straight in the face and check you out."

—Matt Statler, Jackson, Missouri, native

And they like to tell a tall tale now and then . . .

"Missouri grows the biggest liars in the world."

—Vance Randolph, collector of Ozark folklore

"I never, in all my life, had anything whatever to do with robbing any bank in the state of Missouri."

—Cole Younger, member of Jesse James' outlaws

. . . and they are still resourceful and self-reliant.

"It's a do-it-yourself culture."

—David Goodman, St. Louis native

Missouri is a mixture of many things: bustling cities and peaceful meadows, factories and rugged hills. It is a place where cold arctic winds often blow in the winter and where lazily floating down a river is a perfect pastime on hot summer days. Missouri has been called the Gateway to the West, and many of the people who live there continue to enjoy the freedom of wide-open spaces. As a gateway it also has links to the East, especially as seen in St. Louis, with its skyscraper buildings and multicultural atmosphere. Missouri is home to farmers and high-tech innovators, mountain folk absorbed in centuries-old arts and crafts, and university economists. It is these exciting mixtures that make Missouri a great place to live.

Chapter One

In the Heart of the Heartland

The Missouri landscape is like a patchwork quilt with four basic patterns. Rolling grassland covers the state's northern third and a wedge of land along the west. Then to the west is a section of flatlands and gentle hills. In the south, on the Ozark Plateau, the hills are rocky and forested. At the southeastern tip, the Boot Heel, are the swampy lowlands. The official geological names for these areas of the state are the Dissected Till Plains in the north, the Osage Plains in the west, a portion of the Ozark Plateau in much of the southern section, and the Mississippi Alluvial Plain in the southeastern portion.

Taking in all this land together, the state measures almost 300 miles top to bottom and stretches 240 miles east to west. The total area of the state measures 69,704 square miles, making Missouri the twenty-first largest of all the fifty states.

Much of northern Missouri is made up of rolling farmland.

Missouri shares borders with many neighboring states. Arkansas lies to the south, with Iowa on the north, and Illinois, Kentucky, and Tennessee on Missouri's east side. Nebraska, Kansas, and Oklahoma meet the state's western boundary.

DISSECTED TILL PLAINS—GRASSLANDS AND RIVERS

Much of northern Missouri's land is made up of rolling farmland, largely blanketed with green and golden agricultural crops, such as corn, soybeans, and wheat. Its grassy slopes also feed herds of grazing cattle. That area, described by geologists as a dissected till plain, was covered by a glacier thousands of years ago. As the glacier receded, it left behind the fertile soil that is one reason the northern portion of the state is such a good site for farming.

Rivers in this northern section include the Platte, the Grand, and the Chariton, all of which flow south into the Missouri River, which flows west to east, eventually emptying into the Mississippi River. Saint Joseph, Maryville, Kirksville, and Hannibal are cities located in northern Missouri. Kansas City, Missouri's largest city, with an estimated population of more than 450,000, is located in the southwestern corner of the Dissected Till Plains. In 2009 Kansas City was given the honor of being called a tourist "Destination to Watch," a sign that the city is flourishing.

OSAGE PLAINS—FLATLANDS AND GENTLE HILLS

The land south of the Missouri River grows more hilly. This geological region, referred to as the Osage Plains, is located on the western edge of the state. The land there is made up of a combination of flat prairie land and low hills, some of which are topped with yellowish white

The Osage River flows through southern Missouri.

limestone bluffs. Oak trees grow there, along with a short, reddish grass that looks like fox fur. In some places the grasses explode into bloom in the spring and summer. Though the farmland is not as rich as that found in the far north of the state, the Osage Plains is also an agricultural area where corn and other grain crops thrive.

The Osage, the South Grand, and the Blackwater rivers wind through the Osage Plains. Small towns that dot this area include Warrensburg, Belton, Green Ridge, and Sedalia.

OZARK PLATEAU—RUGGED OZARK HILLS

South-central Missouri is a rocky area full of streams, lakes, woods, and caves. This is the Ozark Plateau, an ancient highland of craggy ridges and narrow ravines. It is the largest geological region in Missouri. There is very little level land in the Ozark Plateau. The rugged hills are what give this area its natural beauty. The roads over the Ozark hills are steep and winding. "If you get carsick, it's a terrible place to be," said Matt Statler, recalling family trips through the region.

The downcutting of rivers in the Ozarks has produced deep canyons. Downcutting occurs when a river flows across soft rock,

At Johnson's Shut-Ins State Park, rivers flow over soft rock, forming deep cliffs along riversides.

such as limestone. The river's water, sand, and moving stones carve deeper and deeper into the rock, resulting in steep cliffs with rivers rushing at the bottoms of rocky gorges. Dramatic downcutting can be found at Johnson's Shut-Ins State Park, named for the narrow canyons that enclose its rivers. The rock has been smoothly scooped away by the flowing water. Visitors can slither down these natural waterslides, with or without inner tubes. The "shut-ins" are a favorite destination on hot summer days. "It's full of crazy rock formations," said John Meyer, who grew up nearby.

In the northern Ozarks, near the center of the state, is the Lake of the Ozarks region. Lake of the Ozarks is a sprawling, many-tentacled body of water created by the damming of the Osage River. Other water recreation areas in this section include the Harry S. Truman Reservoir and Table Rock Lake, which is located on the state's southern border. Visitors flock to this popular region to enjoy boating and fishing in a gorgeous setting. Besides the Osage River, there are the Big Piney, the Gasconade, and the Meramec rivers nearby. Jefferson City is the major metropolitan hub in this part of the state as well as Missouri's capital.

Also found in this part of the state are the Saint Francois Mountains, which cover approximately 70 square miles and seem to pop out of the land in small groups of peaks.Taum Sauk Mountain is located among the Saint Francois Mountains. It rises 1,772 feet above sea level—which is not very high as far as mountains go, but is Missouri's highest point. Springfield, Joplin, West Plains, and Farmington are some of the cities located in that part of the state.

Taum Sauk Mountain, at 1,772 feet, is the highest point in Missouri.

MISSISSIPPI ALLUVIAL PLAIN—MISSISSIPPI RIVER BOTTOMLANDS

As you head toward the southeastern corner of the state, the land slopes down to the winding Mississippi River. That declining section is called the Mississippi Alluvial Plain. Though this once was an area of swampy lands, much of it was drained to be used for agriculture. The soil is very rich and good for growing rice and soybeans. In the remaining wild sections the swampy land is home to such plants as foxtail and nut grass, which provide shelter and food for many creatures, including migrating birds. That part of the state is often referred to as the Boot Heel because of the shape of the boundary line.

Towns such as Dexter, Sikeston, Charleston, and Kennett can be found in that southernmost portion of the state. The Mississippi River makes up the eastern boundary of the region.

LIVING WITH FLOODS

Missouri's rivers usually overflow in the spring in their banks when melting snow from the Rocky Mountains flows into tributaries of the state's two largest rivers, the Missouri and the Mississippi. Heavy spring rains also swell the rivers. Though this is a natural process that helps to nurture the soil, the overflowing waters sometimes sweep over

HAZARDS OF THE MISSISSIPPI

The Mississippi River is full of hidden dangers for boats. Large, submerged tree branches, called snags, can catch boats and tear holes in them or tip them over. Boats sometimes run aground on shoals, places where sand and mud have piled up so that they reach almost the surface of the water but are not visible to oncoming navigators.

Another type of rough spot occurs where one river flows into another. For instance, the Missouri River pours into the Mississippi River 10 miles north of downtown St. Louis. The Big Muddy (the nickname for the Missouri River) hits with such force that it crosses the powerful Mississippi River and actually carves a deep notch into the opposite bank before swirling downstream and mixing with the Mississippi.

Father Jacques Marquette, a French missionary who traveled down the Mississippi River in a birchbark canoe in 1673, wrote of this spot: "We were rowing peacefully in clear, calm water when we heard the noise of a rapids into which we were about to fall. I have seen nothing more dreadful. An accumulation of large and entire trees, branches and floating islands was issuing forth from the mouth of the [Missouri] river. . . . We could not without great danger risk passing through it."

farms, drowning chickens, pigs, and cows. Homes and people can also be washed away in heavy flooding. Sometimes whole towns are swamped by the overflow.

In 2008 over abundant rainfall caused considerable damage to homes and farmlands.

Devastating floods struck Missouri in 1993. The Missouri River got so high that after the flooding the people of Rhineland decided to move the whole town. While 157 of the town's residents decided to rebuild their houses on higher ground, one chose to stay in old Rhineland. Eighty-four-year-old Ransom Doll had lived there for almost fifty years and didn't plan on leaving. "My house is built up high," he later explained. "The river only got in my house once in 500 years, back in 1993, and 500 years from now, I don't care how high it gets."

Unfortunately, floods returned to Missouri. In 2007 much of northwestern and central Missouri suffered from excessive rainfall. Then in 2008, after record-breaking rainfalls of more than 10 inches, roads, homes, and farmlands once again were under water, that time in the more southern zones of the state. The Meramec River flowed over major highways, leading President George W. Bush to declare portions of the state, including St. Louis, disaster areas.

LAND AND WATER

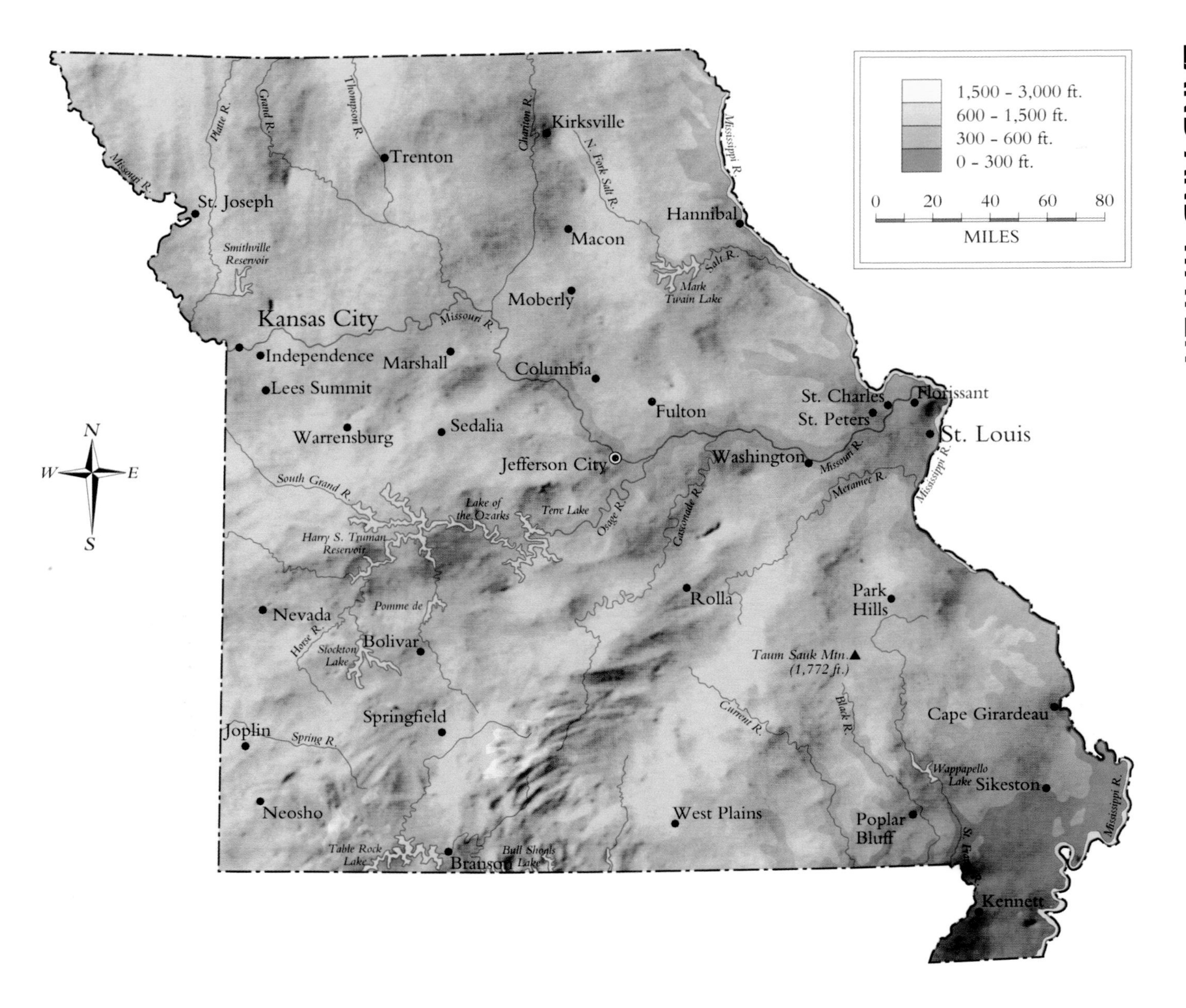

THROUGH THE SEASONS

Missouri offers a pretty complete range of weather. Winters can be harsh but are more often mild. Missouri's snowfalls average 15 inches per year, but even after a heavy snowfall, the snow usually lasts less than a week. Summers, said one St. Louis native, are "hot and humid. . . . The concrete sidewalks stay hot almost until midnight."

Fall can bring rain alternating with cool, sunny, perfect autumn weather. Spring is downright beautiful in Missouri, especially in the Ozarks, where the white-flowered dogwood trees bloom in the fresh woodland air. According to one legend, Missourians in heaven must be tied up. "If they were not chained," related Missouri historian Carl W. Smith, "they would all return to the Ozarks in the spring."

Dogwoods are one of the first signs of spring in the Missouri Ozarks.

MIXED AIRS

High above Missouri, masses of air from other parts of the country collide with one another like a big square dance in the sky. Warm, damp air travels up from the Gulf of Mexico. Air from the Southwest is dry and hot. From the north comes cold Canadian air. When such different air masses crash together, it often causes sudden, sometimes violent, changes in weather.

About the most violent form of weather in Missouri is the tornado, or twister. When a strong updraft of wind hits a whirl of rotating air, a tornado is formed. The funnel-shaped wind mass spins across the ground at speeds of up to 300 miles per hour, destroying everything in its path. The worst tornado ever recorded in the United States passed through Missouri, Illinois, and Indiana on March 18, 1925, killing 695 people and causing millions of dollars worth of damage. Missouri averages between twenty-six and thirty tornadoes a year.

Tornadoes are a weather hazard for the citizens of Missouri.

Sometimes plain windstorms can wreak as much havoc as a twister. After a severe storm, "You'll see some toy you had in your garage in somebody else's yard a mile away," mused one Missouri native. "I saw my sister's umbrella down by the school, a month later."

THE NEW MADRID EARTHQUAKE

When people think of earthquakes in the United States, they most often think of California. But the second-largest earthquake in U.S. history occurred in the middle of the country, in southeastern Missouri! At 2 a.m. on December 16, 1811, an earthquake hit the small river town of New Madrid, jolting sleepers from their beds. People fled from their homes, believing the end of the world had come. Rumbling filled the darkness; houses crashed to their foundations. The earth cracked open, spewing sand and chunks of blackened wood.

On the Mississippi River enormous waves swallowed up islands and riverbanks collapsed, pulling large trees with them. By the next day the river had changed course, and the town was 15 feet farther from the river than before. That earthquake was equivalent to 8 or higher on the Richter scale, and its aftershocks were felt as far away as New York City.

The New Madrid Fault, which caused the 1811 earthquake, underlies a long stretch of the Mississippi River. In fact, minor earthquakes rattle through the area quite frequently, but many are too small even to be felt. Others are noticeable but do not do much damage. One quake in May 1991, measuring 4.6 on the Richter scale, was felt in six states. But it was not serious. "It was a 'dish' tremor," said Robert Latham, a sheriff's dispatcher. "It just shook the dishes."

The variable climate of Missouri is even more unpredictable in the Ozarks, where it can be foggy in one valley and sunny in the next, just a few miles away. One elderly Ozark man said of weather predictions, "Them government weathermen do pretty well on a flat prairie, like Kansas or western Oklahoma, but they ain't worth a damn in a hilly country."

PLANTS AND ANIMALS

Missouri is rich in plant and animal life. The Ozark Mountains' eroded, steep hills and narrow valleys are home to oak and hickory trees, skunk cabbages, bluebells, jack-in-the-pulpits, and wild hyacinths. White-tailed deer, red and gray squirrels, and wild turkeys frequent these forests, feeding on acorns and hickory nuts. Raccoons, opossums, and skunks roam about at night. The rocky Ozark hills are legendary for their poisonous but shy copperhead snakes.

Woodchucks and cottontail rabbits graze in the borders between woods and meadows. In upland meadows, wildflowers like the bright red Indian paintbrush thrive in the thin, rocky soil.

In the bright summer light, wild flowers such as Indian paintbrush grace the open fields.

The rolling meadows in the north-central part of the state are sprinkled with cedar and hardwood trees and teem with birds. Red-tailed hawks coast the sky, watching for white-footed mice on the ground. The prairie is covered with tall grasses and wildflowers where millions of bison once grazed. Some species of grasses grow 10 feet tall, waving in the wind like a strange sea. The prairies are sometimes swathed with white oxeye daisies and bright orange butterfly weed.

Red-tailed hawks help to curtail the populations of mice and other small rodents.

Missouri's rivers, streams, and wetlands abound with fish, turtles, frogs, mussels, beavers, waterbirds, and insects. Along the rivers grow trees like sycamore, cottonwood, silver maple, and box elder. Spring flooding washes away the previous year's dead leaves, leaving a layer of fresh mud where tree seeds sprout and grow. Since the river bottom stays so damp, trees thrive even in years with little rainfall. As a result the bottomlands are often filled with fast-growing forests of towering trees.

CAVES FOR TOURISTS, CAVES FOR BATS

Missouri has an abundance of natural caves—over 5,500—which is more than any other state! In many of these caverns grow bizarre rock formations resembling gigantic icicles, mouthfuls of monstrous teeth, or massive organ pipes. Tourists flock to gaze at these natural wonders. But what's good for tourism isn't necessarily good for the creatures that live in and around the caves.

Bats in particular need caves. Of the fourteen bat species in Missouri, nine live in caves and abandoned mines, hibernating there in the winter. When humans intrude upon their hibernation, the bats fly out of their shelters and die of exposure to the cold. Bats are also left out in the cold when humans seal up their caves and mines. In Missouri the gray bat and the Indiana bat are in danger of extinction. Missouri conservationists and the U.S. government, however, have teamed up to help protect them. They have installed special gates in the openings of abandoned mines that allow bats, but not people, to pass in and out.

The endangered gray bat hibernates in numbers in caves during the winter months.

Chapter Two

Mother of the American West

Missouri has had a turbulent history, and its location is part of the reason. Literally, it has been in the middle of things across the centuries. Its fertile soil has lured settlers since prehistory. Its rivers brought traders, who promoted industry, which in turn provided the home goods to enable people who were even more restless adventurers to move farther west. Those are just some of the ways that Missouri's natural bounty and human enterprise has combined to make it the Mother of the American West.

THE PREHISTORIC PEOPLE

By studying artifacts from the past, archaeologists are able to make educated guesses about the ancient people who lived in the area that is now called Missouri. From such clues the scientists determined that people had inhabited this land for perhaps 12,000 years before Europeans arrived.

By 1820 Missouri had a large enough population to apply for statehood.

One of the first groups of ancient people called the Paleo-Indians, lived in the region from about 12,000 to 8000 BCE. Paleo-Indians probably hunted such large animals as mastodons and woolly mammoths in order to survive. Scientists do not know much about those people, but they have uncovered some of the tools they used. The Dalton Period, which lasted from 7000 to 5000 BCE, is the next cultural division. The Dalton people hunted and also gathered wild fruits and other plants that grew in the area.

The next period is referred to as the Archaic Period and is divided into the Early Archaic, the Middle Archaic, and the Late Archaic time frames, which stretch from about 7000 to 500 BCE. As those thousands of years passed, the people's diet changed. Some caught fish and wild birds; others collected clams and oysters. As the people's diets changed, so too did their tools. Scientists, therefore, can tell, from the shapes of the surviving tools, which period those ancient humans might have lived in and what they ate. By 3000 BCE there were signs that those hunter-gatherers had become less nomadic. They were not constantly on the move, hunting animals. Some bands began to settle down and live in groups, often along the banks of rivers. The Archaic peoples also started weaving cloth and baskets made from natural fibers and, eventually, making pottery.

About one thousand years ago the ancient people began to cultivate their own food crops rather than rely only on the wild plants they found. One of the earliest plants they grew was maize (corn). Trade networks had started to form. Tribes exchanged pottery and beads for other goods with the different groups they came in contact with.

Archaic Indians, one of the earliest inhabitants of present-day Missouri, roasted plant foods and meats over open fires or on rock-lined pits.

THE GREAT VILLAGE

About 1000 CE a great city called Cahokia thrived near present-day St. Louis. The Cahokians hunted deer and bison with stone-tipped arrows and fished with hooks carved from shells. They also farmed corn, beans, and squash. Traveling in canoes, they were part of a trade network that stretched up and down the Mississippi River and its connecting waterways. The Cahokians exchanged salt, corn, and stone tools for copper from the Great Lakes and seashells and sharks' teeth from the Gulf of Mexico.

RIVERSIDE—DEEP IN ANCIENT HISTORY

Riverside is a small town near Kansas City located beside the Missouri River. The history of Riverside is not long in terms of its modern development, but more than two thousand years ago the area was the home of one of the larger groups of ancient people. It is in Riverside that archaeologists have found one of the largest concentrations of artifacts in the entire state of Missouri. The people who might once have lived there are referred to as the Hopewell, also known as the Mound Builders (above). The mounds, most of which have been destroyed, were once all around Riverside. Scientists have learned a little about this ancient culture. The Hopewell people hunted on foot, as horses had not yet been introduced in their area. They also used spears to hunt, because bows and arrows had not yet been invented. By studying the bones left behind, scientists have determined that the diet of the Hopewell included deer, fox, wolf, coyote, beaver, and fish.

The main village that once existed in what has since become Riverside is thought to have covered about 7 acres and was inhabited for approximately 1,500 years. Despite the destruction of the mounds, archaeologists have uncovered thousands of artifacts, which are stored in museums and universities around the state.

Among the amazing remains left by the Cahokians are the large earthen mounds they built. Some of these mounds were constructed as impressive graves for important leaders. Other mounds were likely used for ceremonies, at which Cahokians might worship the sun and other aspects of the natural world. The largest of these mounds, Monks Mound, covers 14 acres and is 100 feet tall. It took three hundred years to build, one basketful of soil at a time.

MODERN NATIVE CULTURE

Over the centuries the mild climate, fertile land, and abundant wildlife of Missouri's river bottomlands attracted other native peoples. The Missouri, Shawnee, Delaware, Piankashaw, Peoria, Iowa, Sauk, and Fox Indians all lived in Missouri at one time or another. The most prominent Missouri-based tribe was probably the Osage, who lived near present-day Jefferson City. Their villages consisted of cone-shaped huts and larger oblong buildings made of poles covered with woven grass. Like the Cahokians, the Osage hunted deer, elk, bison, and bear and planted gardens of corn, beans, and pumpkins.

Members of the Osage tribe were tall, standing more than 6 feet in height.

The Osage were tall, often 6 feet or more, and were fast runners. The men wore red or blue loincloths, with deerskin leggings and moccasins and blankets carried over one shoulder. The women wore wrap skirts, leather tunics and moccasins.

EXPLORERS AND FUR TRADERS

Two of the earliest white people to come to the Missouri area were the French-Canadian explorer Louis Joliet and the French missionary Jacques Marquette. During their 1673 canoe trip down the Mississippi River, they met Peoria Indians, who were friendly and generous, sharing with them a meal of corn, fish, and wild ox.

About a decade later, in 1682, the French explorer René-Robert Cavelier, Sieur de La Salle, stood at the mouth of the Mississippi River and claimed the entire river valley for France. No government official was sent from France, however. Instead, fur trappers and missionaries scouted the region, made maps of its rivers, and traded with the Indians. The French hoped to profit from the area's beavers, muskrats, and otters. Trappers caught these animals and sold their skins to fur traders. The traders shipped big bales of pelts from trading posts along the rivers to the eastern United States and from there to Europe. In 1764 French fur traders Pierre Laclède and Auguste Chouteau founded the village of St. Louis at one of those remote trading posts.

In the late 1700s Spain seized control of the area from France. When France reclaimed it in 1800, the region had more people and more settlements, but otherwise little had changed. French was still the main European language spoken there, and most of the towns' names were French.

MISSOURI TERRITORY

France wasn't sure, though, that it really wanted all that land anyway. Explorers and prospectors had found no gold or silver, and the Indians living there were not always glad to see Europeans. Furthermore,

It was Robert Ford, that dirty little coward,
I wonder how he does feel.
For he ate of Jesse's bread and he slept in Jesse's bed,
And he laid poor Jesse in his grave. *Chorus*

How the people held their breath when they heard of Jesse's death,
And wondered how he ever came to die.
It was one of the gang, called Little Robert Ford,
That shot poor Jesse on the sly. *Chorus*

Jesse was a man, a friend to the poor,
He would never see a man suffer pain.
And with his brother Frank he robbed the Chicago bank,
And stopped the Glendale train. *Chorus*

It was on a Wednesday night, the moon was shining bright,
They stopped the Glendale train.
And the people they did say, for many miles away,
It was robbed by Frank and Jesse James. *Chorus*

They went to a crossing not very far from there,
And there they did the same.
With the agent on his knees, he delivered up the keys
To the outlaws, Frank and Jesse James. *Chorus*

It was on a Saturday night, Jesse was at home,
Talking to his family brave.
Robert Ford came along like a thief in the night,
And laid poor Jesse in his grave. *Chorus*

This song was made by Billy Gashade,
As soon as the news did arrive.
He said there was no man with the law in his hand,
Who could take Jesse James while alive. *Chorus*

Being a border state between the North and the South, Missouri was trapped in the middle of the war. Large-scale battles between Union and Confederate armies raged inside its borders of the state. There were 1,162 battles and skirmishes fought in Missouri, the third-highest number of any state. Meanwhile, William C. Quantrill, a notorious Confederate captain, with his gang of proslavery ruffians, wreaked havoc, burning houses, looting towns, and killing Union sympathizers. Missouri-born Jesse James rode with Quantrill's raiders. After the war he became a famous outlaw with a gang of his own.

Shortly before the war ended, in 1865, slavery in Missouri was abolished. More than 100,000 African-American men, women, and children in Missouri were freed. Many were also left homeless and jobless.

Some African Americans moved to large cities, where they had a chance of finding work in mills and factories, or as housemaids and other servants. Some moved north. Most, however, lacking the resources to move away, stayed where they were, often living in horrible poverty. Some continued working for the same landowners who had once owned them, for wages that allowed them a life a little better than that of salves. As one former slave put it, they now had "nothing but freedom."

On August 10, 1861, the Battle of Wilson's Creek, also known as the Battle of Oak Hills, was fought between Union forces and the Missouri State Guard.

The Civil War changed many things. Throughout the war Missouri's trade with the South stopped, including its river trade.

In 1817 cheering crowds had greeted the *Zebulon Pike* when it became the first steamboat to splash up the Mississippi River from New Orleans to St. Louis. Soon many steamboats plied the river. At the time riverboats were the cheapest way to transport heavy goods and did it faster than shipping overland.

St. Louis was an important port for riverboat traffic along the Mississippi River.

Since it cost money and time to send raw materials to the east to be processed, mills were built along the Mississippi River. Flour and lumber mills sprang up in Hannibal and other towns to grind grain from Iowa, and to cut logs from Wisconsin and Minnesota.

Thrifty riverboats were not a perfect means of transport, however. They frequently capsized on the treacherous rivers. Collisions, explosions, groundings, and impacts with submerged logs and rocks all took their toll. Accidents wrecked about 30 percent of all steamboats built before 1849.

In 1851 railroad construction began in Missouri. Over the next decade railroads crisscrossed the state and connected Missouri with the East and West coasts. Trains were faster than barges or steamboats, and they could go where boats could not. The steamboat, once a symbol of progress and prosperity for towns along the big rivers, became a relic of a bygone era.

ST. LOUIS AND THE GILDED AGE

In Missouri all railroads led to St. Louis. In the early nineteenth century the city had grown from a small fur-trading post into a thriving metropolis. By 1850 its mills were producing half a million barrels of flour a year. The city also exported bacon, beef, corn, oats, and apples. Some factories made steamboat engines, iron stoves, ornamental ironwork, and lead pipe. Others brewed beer or wove cotton and wool into cloth. Great waves of immigrants from Germany, Ireland, Italy, and Czechoslovakia supplied St. Louis with the cheap labor, skilled workers, and businesspeople to drive the busy city.

St. Louis also profited in the 1840s and 1850s from the movement of settlers seeking fortunes that they hoped lay farther west. The city's entrepreneurs outfitted those travelers with clothing, food, tools, and machinery. As it continued to mother the West, St. Louis itself flourished. A building boom created civil and cultural institutions. St. Louis University was established in 1832, and in 1839 the University of Missouri was founded in Columbia—the first state university west of the Mississippi River. During the 1850s the river city also instituted a public school system.

By the 1870s St. Louis had grown into a major manufacturing city with a population of almost half a million. But all that growth came at a cost. The noises, smells, and wastes of progress overwhelmed the city.

The need for steel during World War II helped to boost Missouri's economy.

Factories, fueled by coal, spewed noxious black smoke from their chimneys. Factory owners were growing rich, but the people laboring in the factories were paid very little and remained abjectly poor, packed into crowded slums. "Greater futures enjoyed by a few—hard times suffered by many" was a common saying.

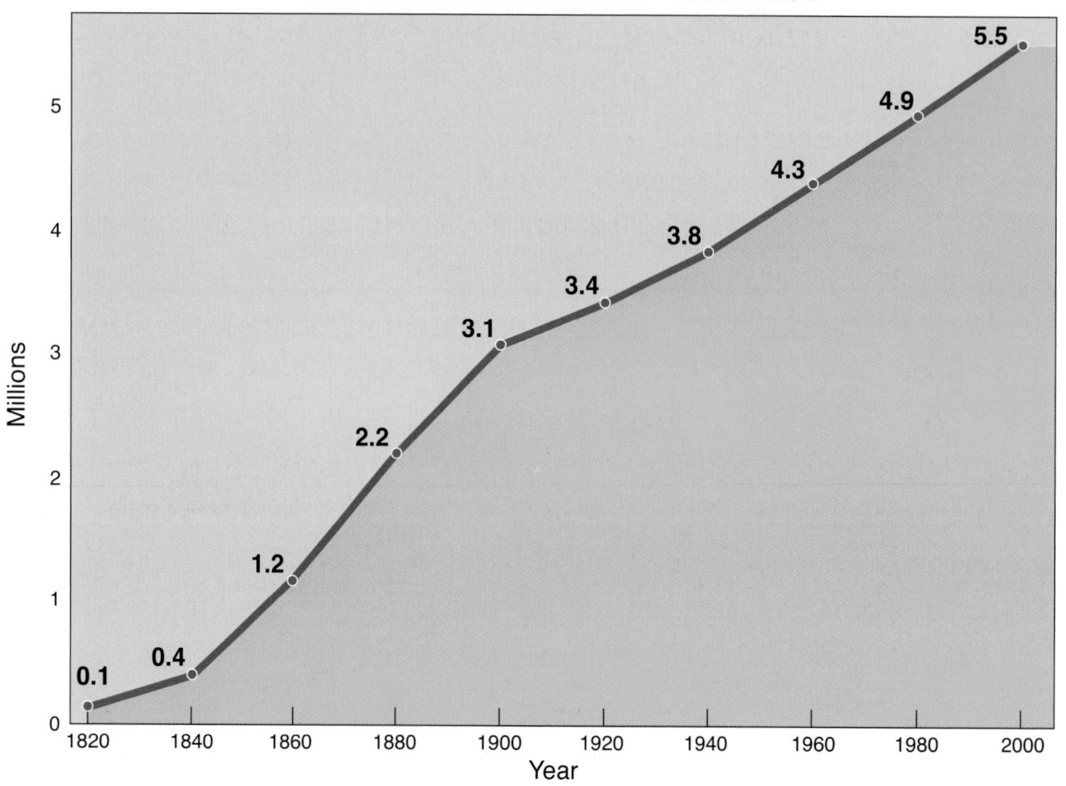

The late nineteenth century was called the Gilded Age, because it was a time when expensive decoration was camouflaging decay and misery. Missouri author Mark Twain wrote cynically in 1871, "What is the chief end of man?—to get rich. In what way?—dishonestly, if we can; honestly if we must." Many ambitious folks in St. Louis seemed to make those words their motto. By the turn of the twentieth century St. Louis had gained a reputation for appalling political corruption, with city officials often accepting bribes from businesses. In the process the rich got richer and the poor got poorer.

THE TWENTIETH CENTURY

Even so, turn-of-the-century St. Louis had a promising future. The 1904 world's fair at St. Louis wowed the entire country with its spectacular exhibits and innovations. Missouri's other big city, Kansas City, was also flourishing, providing the country with hogs, cattle, wheat, and soybeans. Across the state, universities and public libraries were founded; dams, bridges, and roads were built.

But then, like the rest of America, Missouri sank into the Great Depression of the 1930s. Unemployment skyrocketed as businesses closed. A scorching drought dried up crops and killed livestock. Farm prices fell, wages were slashed, banks failed, and people grew hungry—and anguished. It was bad all over. The state of Missouri coped with the help of federally funded relief programs. For example, a federal project resettled displaced farmers on government farmland, loaning them money for food, livestock, and seeds.

But things did not start to look up until 1941, when the United States entered World War II, and farms and factories geared up for the war effort. In 1945 Missourian Harry S. Truman became vice president. With the death of President Franklin D. Roosevelt three months later, Truman was suddenly faced with the presidency—and the task of ending the war. In August 1945 he ordered the U.S. military to drop two atomic bombs on Japan, demolishing the cities of Hiroshima and Nagasaki and killing 96,000 civilians. Many more died slowly from radiation poisoning. Some people believe that even more lives were saved, both American and Japanese, by ending the war quickly.

By that time the manufacturing sector had replaced agriculture as Missouri's main employer. Missouri was quickly becoming an urban state.

THE ST. LOUIS EXPO

Skate on an ice rink through an artificial blizzard—in the middle of summer! Send a telegraph message to a city 1,500 miles away! Gaze upon the first moving pictures you have ever seen, and catch a glimpse of life in exotic, far-off lands. At the St. Louis World's Fair, also called the Louisiana Purchase Exposition, people saw Eskimo igloos, Zuñi cliff dwellings, and real live yodelers from the Tyrolean Alps. Those things are unremarkable today, but in 1904 they were astonishing. As a visitor with the nineteenth century still fresh in your mind, the 1904 world's fair had almost everything you could think of—and many things you couldn't.

The fair celebrated the one hundredth anniversary of the Louisiana Purchase and the accomplishments of St. Louis and the Midwest. Elaborately ornamented buildings were constructed and filled with the latest innovations and glimpses of cultures from around the world. Eye-catching displays showed off the state's best in agriculture, livestock, mining, and fine arts.

At the fair visitors bit into the first hot dogs served in buns, sipped the first iced tea, and tasted the first cotton candy, then called fairy floss. And it was there, too, that an imaginative waffle vendor packed ice cream into a thin, rolled waffle, creating the first ice cream cone.

The exposition brought St. Louis to the attention of the world. Sometimes it seemed everyone was singing "Meet me in St. Louis, Louis, meet me at the Fair," lyrics from a newly popular tune.

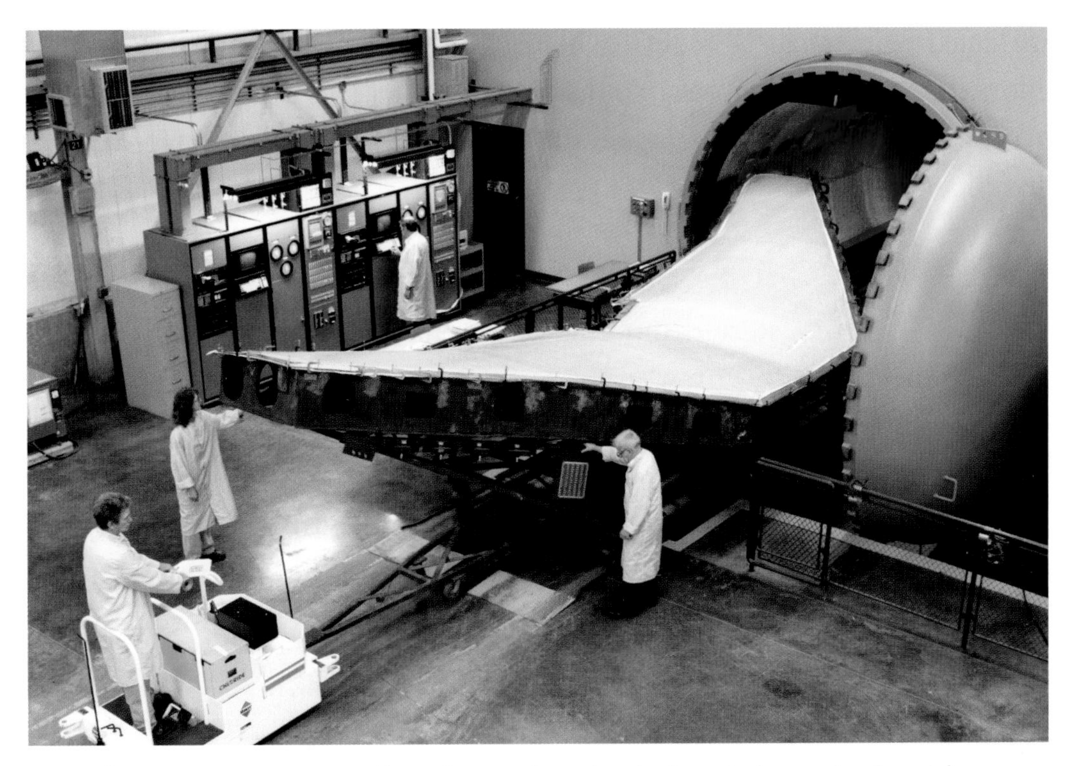

Agriculture gives way to manufacturing, such as the airplane industry, by the mid–twentieth century.

By 1970 almost 75 percent of Missourians lived in cities and towns. In the 1980s Missouri moved into high-technology manufacturing, which included the pharmaceutical and aerospace industries. Other changes in the Missouri economy included the buildup of the service industry, which took over as the leading industry in the state. There were more people working in places such as restaurants, hospitals, and insurance companies, for instance, than there were in manufacturing. Recreational areas, created near artificial lakes in the southern half of the state, attracted tourists to Missouri, which also added to the state's economy. Nonetheless, the economy would falter in the 1980s, due in part to a national recession that caused the loss of jobs and other hardships for Missourians.

THE TWENTY-FIRST CENTURY

The new century started out nicely for many Missourians, as the St. Louis Rams football team won the Super Bowl in 2000. "The town went nuts," wrote a reporter for the Associated Press. It was the first Super Bowl win for the city. Two years later the Rams were not so lucky. They made it to the Super Bowl again but lost in a tight game to the New England Patriots in 2002.

Six years later Missouri came in last. That time it was not in a game of football or any other sport. Rather, in 2008, Missouri was the last state to officially register the number of votes that its citizens had cast in the presidential election. A record-breaking number of Missourians came out to vote (almost 3 million people), and in the end the difference between the winner and the loser was fewer than four thousand votes. As a result, it took officials extra time to make sure the count was accurate. It turned out to be only the second time, since 1904, that Missourians did not choose the candidate who would go on to win the U.S. presidency. A slim majority of Missourians had voted for John McCain, while the national winner turned out to be Barack Obama.

As the new U.S. president was preparing to take office, the country was shaken by incredibly bad economic news. Banks were closing. Homeowners were forced into bankruptcy. People by the thousands were losing jobs. The economy was in a recession, and it was affecting Missouri. Though many people in the nation were suffering greatly, Missourians were holding their own. Because Missouri's economy is more diversified than many other states', there was hope in 2009 that Missouri would not be hit as hard by the economic disaster as some neighboring states had been.

Missouri's legislature, along with the citizens who elected them, was hopeful that Missouri would be able to stay strong. People looked favorably toward the unfolding of the twenty-first century.

Chapter Three

Middle Americans

Missouri is smack-dab in the middle of the country—sort of. At least, it's caught in the middle. Sandwiched between distinct regions of the United States, it shares traits with the states it rubs shoulders with. At one time St. Louis stood for the industrial East and Kansas City for the Wild West. Today, St. Louis is still characterized by manufacturing (enabling an urban, eastern lifestyle), and Kansas City is yet a major grain and livestock market (indicating a western, prairie kind of life). The stereotypes of the past, however, have matured and blended into a population from all walks of life enjoying a variety of styles.

THE STATE OF THE STATE

The U.S. Census Bureau estimated in 2008 that Missouri's total population was 5,911,605. Of this total the majority is white. The largest minority group is African American, which numbers 677,657. The next largest minority is Hispanic, at 178,421, making up about 3 percent of the state's population. The majority of Hispanics in Missouri come from Mexico.

Many Missourians in the western part of the state still look to agriculture for a lifestyle.

Missouri's population is one of diversity.

Asian Americans come in third, at 85,505, and American Indians number 29,060. A total of 80,767 people in Missouri identify themselves as being more than one race.

More than half of Missourians live in urban areas now, and the number of people living on farms is rapidly declining. City dwellers are moving to suburbs, and newcomers to Missouri tend to settle in its popular recreational areas, especially around the beautiful Lake of the Ozarks region.

IMMIGRANTS, OLD AND NEW

The first Europeans to settle in what is now Missouri were French. They began building towns there in the eighteenth century, when the area was still under French authority. Sainte Genevieve, founded in the early 1700s, was the territory's first permanent European settlement. A big

ETHNIC MISSOURI

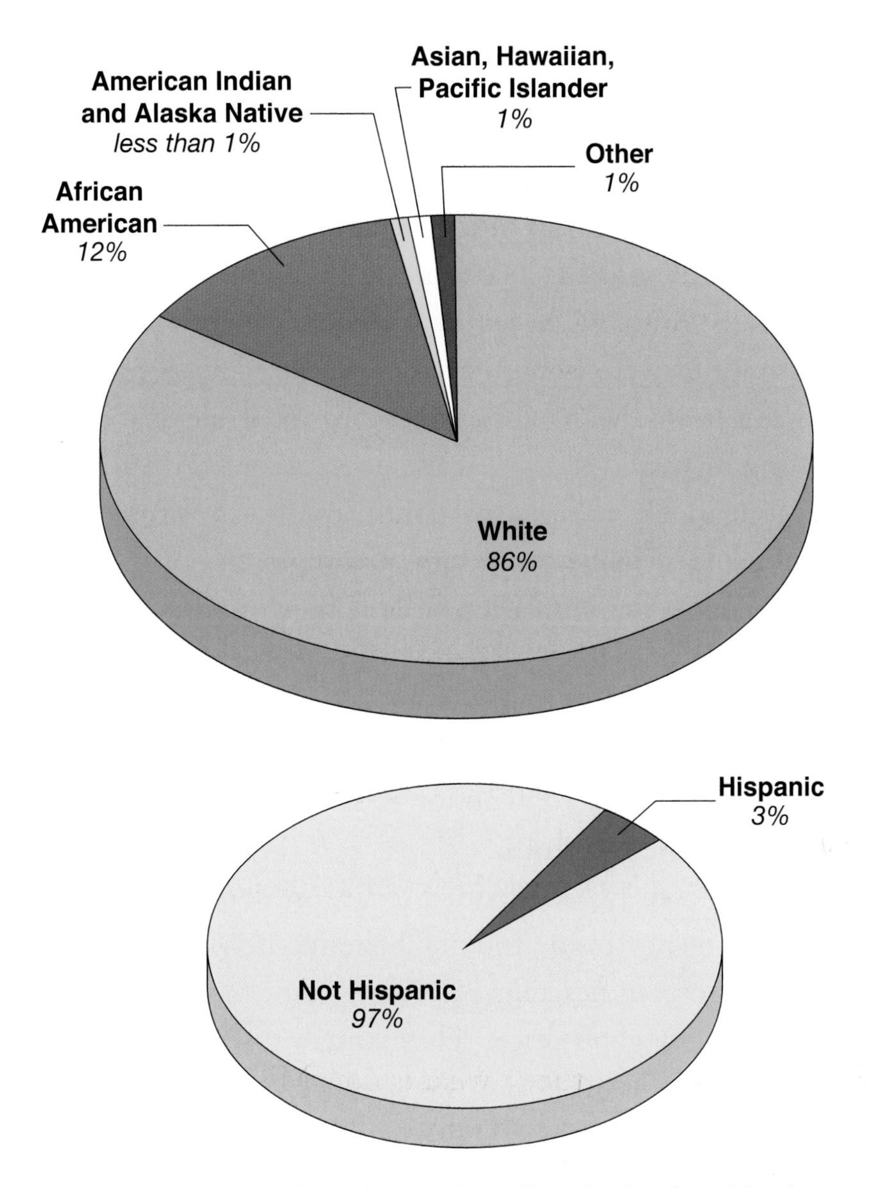

Note: A person of Cuban, Mexican, Puerto Rican, South or Central American, or other Spanish culture or origin, regardless of race, is defined as Hispanic.

event in Sainte Genevieve today is the French Heritage Festival in June. It features traditional music and an emphasis on the town's eighteenth-century French colonial history. "Why do people traipse to Williamsburg [Virginia] when there is such wonderful colonial history here?" asks Carl J. Ekberg, an expert on the local French architecture. According to Ekberg, Sainte Genevieve has more French buildings than New Orleans, Louisiana, a city famous for its charming French district.

By the early nineteenth century Missouri belonged to the United States. Its factories were booming, and people were needed to work in them. As Europeans heard about the jobs available in Missouri, they began coming in great waves to escape poverty, hunger, and political and religious intolerance in their native countries. It was during this time that St. Louis blossomed into a huge city, rivaling some of the cities on the East Coast in size. The population of St. Louis increased more than 230 percent in one decade, from 1810 to 1820. Between the 1830s and the 1860s the city's population doubled every ten years.

The greatest numbers of immigrants in the mid–1800s came from Ireland and Germany. By 1850 about 40 percent of the population of St. Louis was from those countries.

Immigrants from Ireland tended to live in two areas of St. Louis, in Kerry Patch on the north side and in Cheltenham. Many Irish immigrants found jobs in the clay mines. Some Germans came to farm the land that was being offered at very good prices. Hermann, a town in a lush river valley about 45 miles west of St. Louis, was settled by the German immigrants who arrived between 1830 and 1870. Many German farmers grew fruits, especially grapes, berries, and apples. The soil was excellent for grape growing, and the town became known for its excellent German wines.

In St. Louis many celebrate Oktoberfest with authentic German foods, music, and dance.

Oktoberfest is a celebration of that German heritage. It is held every weekend in October in Hermann, when people get together to taste the local wines, eat their fill of hearty German food, and get an earful of authentic German music.

As the demand for factory workers increased, Missouri witnessed another surge of immigration from other European countries. A lack of work in Europe in the 1880s released a flood of immigrants to the St. Louis area. Job seekers from Scotland, Belgium, Wales, Switzerland, Portugal, Italy, and Czechoslovakia began arriving with their families in the late 1800s. Many of the new arrivals worked in cotton factories and in breweries, where beer was made. Their working and living conditions were far from ideal. They worked long hours for poor pay and could afford to live only in tenement houses, which were poorly built and maintained, and very crowded.

By the mid–1890s the St. Louis neighborhood that came to be called the Hill was almost entirely Italian. Many Italians who had worked in clay mines in Italy took jobs in St. Louis's brick factories or in nearby clay, lead, and coal mines. That neighborhood is where Lawrence "Yogi" Berra grew up. Berra was a Yankee's catcher legendary for his amusing sayings, like "If people don't want to come out to the ballpark, nobody is going to them."

The nineteenth century also brought new arrivals from other states, especially from the South. Some moved to Missouri during the Civil War. Others moved later to find jobs. Freed blacks, though still discriminated against, found slightly better living conditions and chances for employment in Missouri than they had in the South. New Englanders, following the lure of the West, came in search of land to buy on the legendary plains.

Today, Missouri's new immigrant population is not huge, but it's getting larger, especially in St. Louis. Since the 1960s the city has received a stream of Vietnamese immigrants. Other Southeast Asians—from Thailand, Laos, and the Philippines—have also arrived. Today the community around South Grand Boulevard is full of Asian and Hispanic restaurants, grocery stores, and bakeries. Many of the community's immigrants came to Missouri as political refugees, escaping wars and political upheavals in their home countries.

St. Louis's growing Hispanic community is centered in the neighborhood around Cherokee and Iowa streets. Three of the nearby Roman Catholic churches offer masses in Spanish. Mexican grocery stores and restaurants fill the area's aging red-brick buildings. On May 5 of each year the community celebrates Cinco de Mayo—a beloved Mexican holiday recalling the Mexican victory over the French at Puebla in 1862.

POPULATION DENSITY

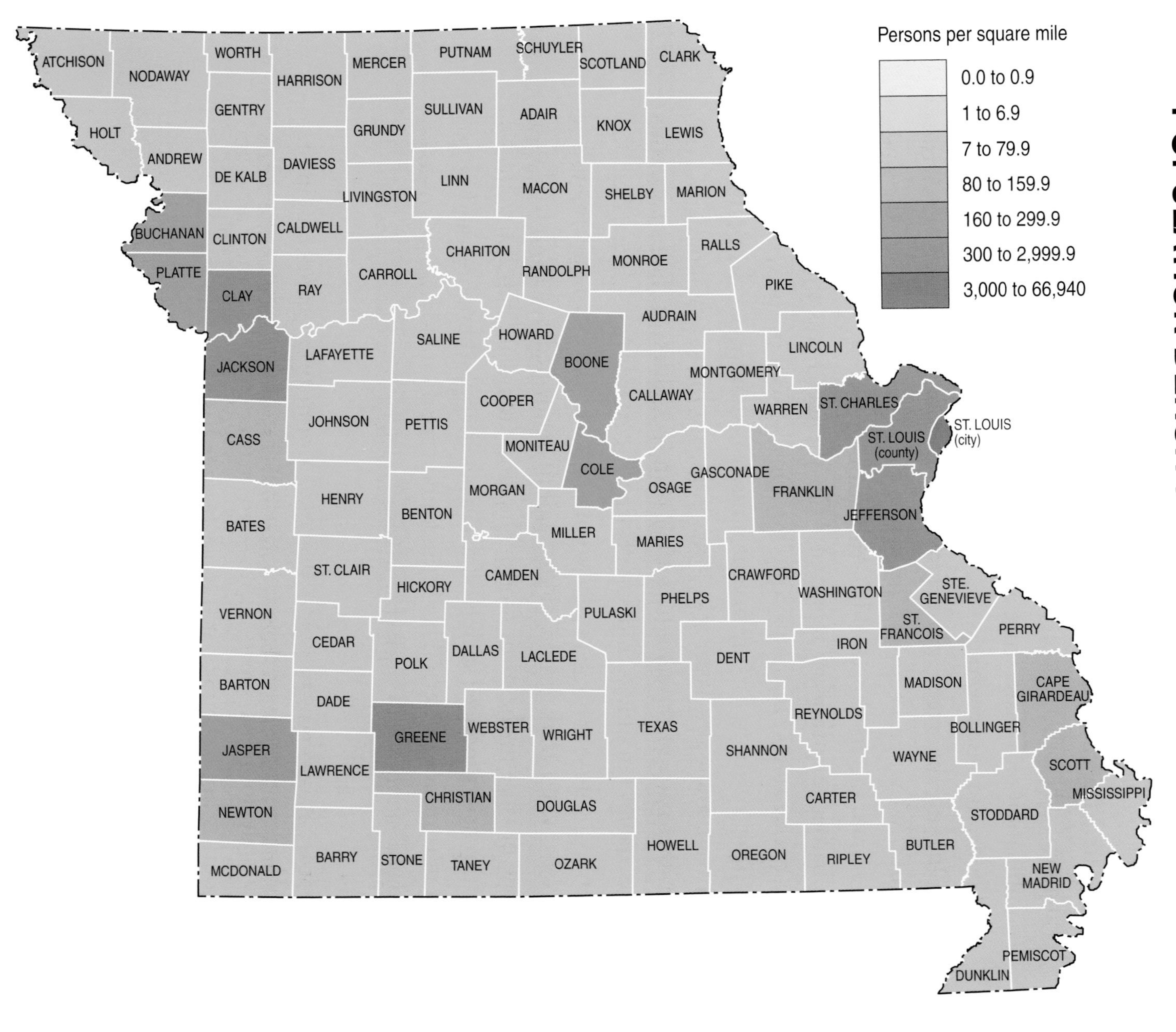

BARBECUE AND OTHER GOOD THINGS TO EAT

Kansas City has been called the Barbecue Capital of the World. Two things make its barbecue sauce distinctive. One is the addition of vinegar for tanginess. The other, according to barbecue aficionado Rich Davis, is its combination of tomato sauce and hot pepper "with molasses for character and body, not just sweetness."

One of the city's most famous barbecue restaurants is Arthur Bryant's. Writer and Kansas City native Calvin Trillin titled it "the single best restaurant in the world." American presidents have eaten there. One barbecue enthusiast reported, "On the day I was there, I saw cars from twelve states" in the parking lot. On the wall of the restaurant is a newspaper cartoon. Arthur Bryant himself is standing at the pearly gates of heaven, and Saint Peter asks him, "Did you bring any sauce?"

Other parts of the state have their own specialties. St. Louis is famous for its Italian restaurants and superb frozen custard. At a place called Ted Drewes, the ice cream–type dessert is so thick that St. Louisians call it concrete. The Ozark region of the state is renowned for its down-home cuisine of close-to-the-earth foods. The area's abundant fish, game, herbs, and fruit have produced such local delicacies as apple dumplings and catfish fried in cornmeal batter. "This is the kind of food Grandma used to do on Sundays," reminisced Ozark chef Moose Zader.

CARDINALS, RAMS, ROYALS, AND CHIEFS, JUST TO START WITH

Every state loves its sports teams—no matter how bad they are—and Missouri is no exception. St. Louis's former baseball team, the St. Louis Browns, was a terrible team for years and years. They finally made it to the

Despite the invasion of the modern world in the form of automobiles, television, and the Internet, some traditional folk arts have survived, such as fiddle playing, quilt making, and wood carving. So has the tendency to tell folktales that are amusing, vivid, and usually unbelievable. In the 1930s and 1940s there was even a club of old pranksters called the Post, whose sole purpose was to play jokes on strangers, making them believe outrageous falsehoods.

Missouri tall tales frequently have to do with the plentiful hunting and fishing opportunities in the Ozarks' valleys and forests. Stories of outrunning wolves, killing bears with a jackknife, shooting one hundred ducks with a single load of shot—anything is possible, said writer Frederick Simpich. "They don't expect you to believe, but they do like you to laugh and appreciate their storytelling powers."

Whether working hard, playing hard, or laughing hard, the people of Missouri know how to come together and enjoy a good summer day, a night watching a baseball game, or a weekend at one of the state's many fairs.

Chapter Four

The Government

All American states are united under the U.S. government, but every state also has its own government. Missouri's government is based on its constitution, which was first written in 1820. This constitution has been amended, or changed, several times, when Missourians felt that their basic laws should be adapted to new circumstances. The Missouri state motto is "The welfare of the people shall be the supreme law."

INSIDE GOVERNMENT

Missouri's state government is divided into three parts: executive, legislative, and judicial.

Executive

The executive branch includes the governor, the lieutenant governor, and other elected and appointed officials. The governor is responsible for making the budget for the state and has the power to sign into law or veto (reject) bills passed by the state legislature. The governor is elected to a four-year term.

Missouri's Capitol, completed in 1917, houses the two legislative bodies and provides office space for the governor, lieutenant governor, secretary of state, treasurer, auditor, and some administrative agencies.

Every four years Missourians vote for a new governor, such as Jeremiah W. (Jay) Nixon, elected in 2008.

Legislative

The legislative branch makes the laws of the state by writing bills and voting on them. The Missouri legislature has a 34-member senate and a 163-member house of representatives.

Judicial

Missouri's judicial system has three levels. At the lowest level are the circuit courts, commonly known as trial courts. At the next level is the court of appeals, which may review decisions made by the circuit courts. At the top is the state supreme court, the final authority on Missouri law. Missouri's supreme court has seven judges, each of whom may serve one twelve-year term, except for the chief justice, who may serve two. The judges are first appointed by the governor from nominations submitted by a judicial selection committee. After judges serve one year, the state's citizens vote on whether they should remain on the court.

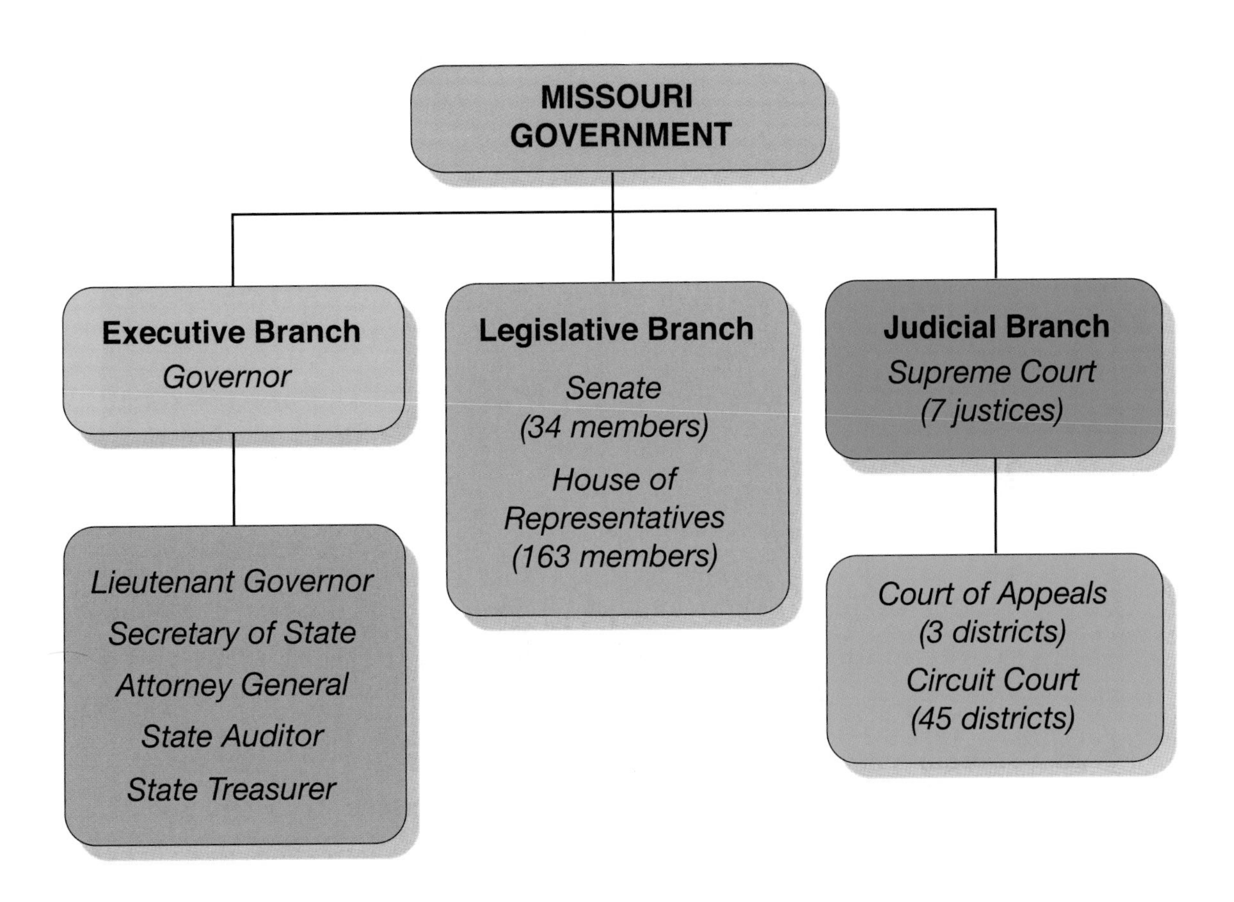

PROVIDING TRANSPARENCY IN MISSOURI'S STATE GOVERNMENT

In 2007 then-governor Matt Blunt created an initiative that increased both the transparency and the accountability of the state government. To provide tax payers easy access to information on how much tax money the state was using and where the money was going, a website was created. The site is called the Missouri Accountability Portal (MAP), and in its first year online, it recorded more than 10 million hits.

Through the MAP website, anyone can learn where Missourians' taxes are going. This not only provides people with an understanding of how their taxes are being used, but it also makes state legislators more careful about how they spend the state's money. "With this important resource," Governor Blunt stated before leaving office, "Missourians can map their tax dollars and hold their elected officials accountable for their spending choices."

To ensure that the information on the website is current, figures are updated at the close of every business day. The data provided includes the salaries of state employees, as well as a list of businesses that have failed to pay state taxes. The MAP database is one of the first of its kind in all the states to go online, and it's a way of keeping Missourians informed about their state government's business.

THE VOICE OF THE PEOPLE

Missourians have always wanted a say in their government. Two ways they can change the constitution are by initiative and referendum. If enough citizens sign a petition, a proposed change or initiative can be put on the ballot, so people can vote on it. A referendum goes through a similar process, but the purpose of a referendum is to allow voters to get rid of an existing law.

An example of how this works involves a gambling issue tied with an education issue. In 2009 fees levied on Missouri's casinos provided more than $130 million for the state's schools, but there remained debate about how the money would be spent. So for people interested in education, any proposed changes in the gambling law would be important ones that merit their appearances on ballots.

In the 1990s riverboat gambling stirred up a lot of attention when a referendum was put on the voting ballot. According to Missouri's constitution, gambling can only be conducted on the Mississippi and Missouri rivers. Hoping to comply with the law, some owners of gambling boats who didn't actually want their boats to be on the river created artificial ponds right next to the river. They connected the ponds to the river by ditches or water pipes, thinking this would be legal. They ran into trouble, however, when the Missouri Supreme Court ruled that their artificial basins violated the constitution. The law stated that the boats should be on the river, and those particular boats definitely were not. When casino owners complained, the question of the so-called boats in moats was put to the people as a referendum.

MISSOURI BY COUNTY

Those in favor of changing the constitution so the boats could stay in the ponds said that the casinos brought jobs to the community. They also pointed out how much of the casinos' money was used to support the public schools. But opponents protested that the amount of money that actually got to the schools was insignificant. "The total gambling tax dollars that support education in Missouri are equal to one textbook per child in Missouri," one report noted. Those voters also objected that most of the casino jobs paid little more than minimum wage. Furthermore, studies showed that 5 percent of gamblers become addicted to gambling. Some lost all their money, their jobs, and sometimes their families, too, when they could not stop gambling. Thus, in their minds, gambling brought more trouble than support for the community. "Gambling brings false hope, distress . . . crime," stated Greg Holley, a St. Louis minister and recovered gambler.

Riverboat casinos help to bring in tourists and boost the state's economy.

The casino industry spent almost $10 million to persuade voters to allow casinos to float in the man-made basins. In 1994, 56 percent of the people who voted in the referendum said yes, so the casinos were allowed to operate in the moats. As of 2008 there were eleven Missouri-approved casinos in the state, employing almost 11,000 people. The citizens of the state had the last word on that issue.

SEED
CORN
ASGROW.

Chapter Five

The Economy

Luckily, gambling isn't the only way to make money in Missouri. The mainstay of the state's economy lies in the service industries, manufacturing, and agriculture. Though the state's economy suffered in 2009, affected by the declining U.S. economy, Missouri was doing better than many of the other states in that time of economic problems.

Despite this, the gross state product, the amount of goods and services that creates the economy, increased slightly in 2008. One of the areas that was doing best was the export business. That was because the cost of U.S. products was exceptionally low in other countries (due to the international decline in the value of the U.S. dollar). Thus foreign companies were eager to buy Missouri products, and the volume of sales was breaking state records.

MISSOURI'S SERVICE INDUSTRY LEADS THE ECONOMY

Accounting for around 40 percent of Missouri's economy, the service industry includes companies and businesses that exist to help people.

Corn is one of Missouri's biggest cash crops.

Many of Missouri's professional sports teams, such as the Kansas City Royals, bring in lots of money to the state.

This includes retail stores that sell clothes and other products. Doctors, nurses, and therapists are also a part of the service industry. So too are hotels, restaurants, and movie theaters; lawyers, engineers, and professional athletes. Missouri's sports teams bring in a lot of money to the state. Banks, real estate, and insurance companies are also included in this sector of the state's economy. As a matter of fact, those last three types of businesses make one of the biggest contributions of all to the state's economy.

Another large category of the service industry is government—meaning that teachers and other people who work in Missouri's schools are included in this sector, as are the state's politicians and military personnel. Government is the fourth-largest service industry in Missouri.

People who work in transportation include bus drivers, train and bus station workers, and those who work on the many barges that ply Missouri's waterways. Communications is another part of the service industry. That includes telephone, radio, and television companies.

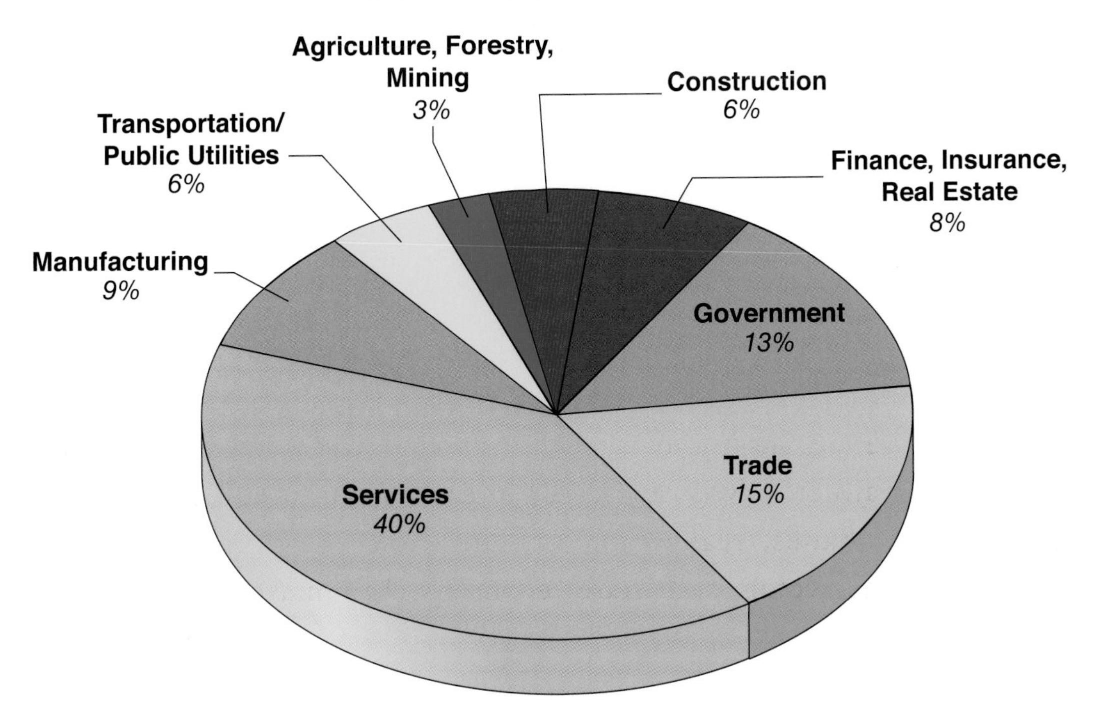

ENCOURAGING NEW TYPES OF INDUSTRIES

In the past couple of decades, people have been moving out of the crowded cities into the suburbs. Overcrowding was one of the reasons, but another reason was to go to work for new industries that have been steadily coming to the state. A good example is what happened in St. Charles County, west of St. Louis.

It was there that the credit-card corporation MasterCard decided to locate its Global Technology and Operations Center. The telecommunications company MCI WorldCom soon followed, establishing a regional center there. "High-tech companies tend to cluster together," said Rick Finholt, director of the Missouri Research Park in St. Charles County. "Once you establish the cluster, others join."

Sure enough, in the 1990s, fifteen companies moved to the area. Developers were optimistic about the high-tech economic expansion in the region. "This is the direction growth is going in St. Louis," Finholt said. "We're in the path of growth." Such growth has continued, though the economic slowdown in 2008 and 2009 also affected the high-tech industry. But in 2007 Novus International, a global animal health and nutrition company, constructed a $20 million building there. And there's still room for many more new high-tech businesses.

MANUFACTURING COMES IN SECOND

A large share of Missouri's seven thousand (or more) manufacturing factories is concentrated in or near its two biggest cities, St. Louis and Kansas City. Before Missouri was even a state, St. Louis was already manufacturing shoes, furniture, pottery, bricks, and beer. By 1850 St. Louis was well established as an industrial center. In fact, after baseball became popular in the late 1800s, St. Louis was jokingly ranked "first in booze, first in shoes, and last in the American League."

2007 GROSS STATE PRODUCT: $229 Million

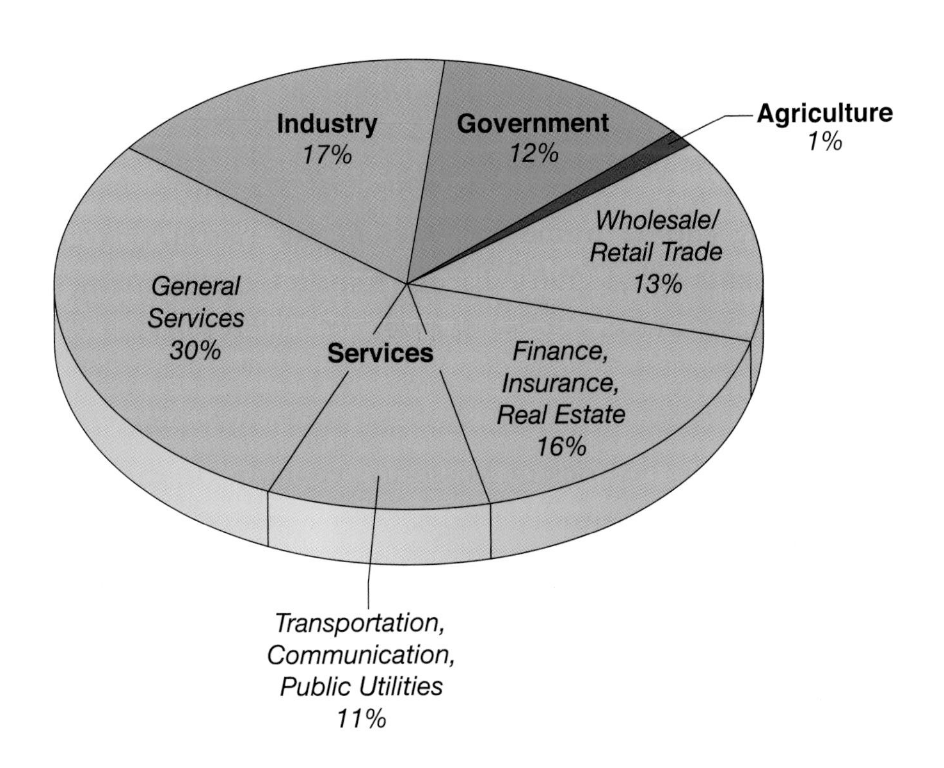

Today's St. Louis retains much of its manufacturing legacy. Among its major industries are the Anheuser-Busch brewery, which produces almost half the beer consumed in the United States, and the pet food producer Ralston-Purina. Another important manufacturing employer is the chemical company Monsanto, a pioneer in genetically engineered crops, developed to resist diseases and pests. The production of chemicals is the state's leading manufacturing activity. In St. Louis numerous chemical products, such as fertilizers, paint, and insecticides, are made. Pharmaceuticals are manufactured mostly in Kansas City laboratories. Kansas City is also the corporate headquarters of the monolithic greeting card company Hallmark, started almost one hundred years ago.

Other manufactured products include transportation equipment. One of the biggest producers is Boeing, the airplane maker. Trucks are also produced in the state, as are busses, barges, and railroad cars. Food processing is another big part of Missouri's manufacturing sector. Springfield is home to one of the nation's largest dairy-processing plants called Prairie Farms. Kansas City has many large flour mills that process wheat.

AGRICULTURE—SMALL FARMS AND BIG PROBLEMS

Agriculture was the bedrock of Missouri's economy in the 1800s. Today the state continues to produce hogs, beef cattle, soybeans, and corn. But with the state's manufacturing and service economies on the rise, fewer and fewer Missourians make their living as farmers. Large, high-production farms are also responsible for elbowing out small farmers, and the family farm is rapidly becoming a thing of the past.

The airplane manufacturer, Boeing, provides jobs for about 35,000 Missourians.

Such megafarms are often combined with processing plants. For instance, many meatpacking companies own and raise the hogs they process into pork. That means they buy fewer hogs from independent farmers. Since big factory farms make more money than small ones, they are better able to survive economic setbacks like falling prices. They also purchase supplies at cheaper prices because they buy them in such large quantities, giving them an edge that smaller farmers cannot compete with.

A DIFFERENT KIND OF LIVESTOCK

Farmers pushed out of hog, soybean, and corn farming by large producers sometimes turn to more specialized farming. Beekeeping, crayfish farming, and raising Christmas trees are some of the less conventional ways Missouri's small farmers are making a living.

Elk once roamed wild in Missouri, and they are coming back—except they're on farms now. Terry Furstenau raises elk in Fayette. What started as a whim became a successful herd of fifty animals. Elk eat half as much feed as cattle, and they browse on native Missouri grasses. "It took more work to keep fifteen cattle alive during the winter than it did to keep fifty elk alive all year," said Furstenau.

Furstenau and others—about one hundred people in Missouri—raise elk not so much for their meat as for the velvet that grows anew on their antlers every year. The biggest market for the velvet is in Korea, where it is valued as a medicine.

The number of small, family-owned farms is diminishing as corporate farms take control of Missouri agriculture.

The number of Missouri's small, independent farms has been steadily decreasing. About two-thirds of the state is still considered farmland, however, consisting of more than 100,000 farms. Those farms, big and small, are some of the greatest producers in the nation of cattle, hogs, and turkeys. Other animals that are raised in great numbers are chickens and sheep. Farmers also grow crops, such as soybeans, corn, wheat, and sorghum (another type of cereal grass). Most of those crops are not sold in grocery stores for human consumption. Rather, they are

EARNING A LIVING

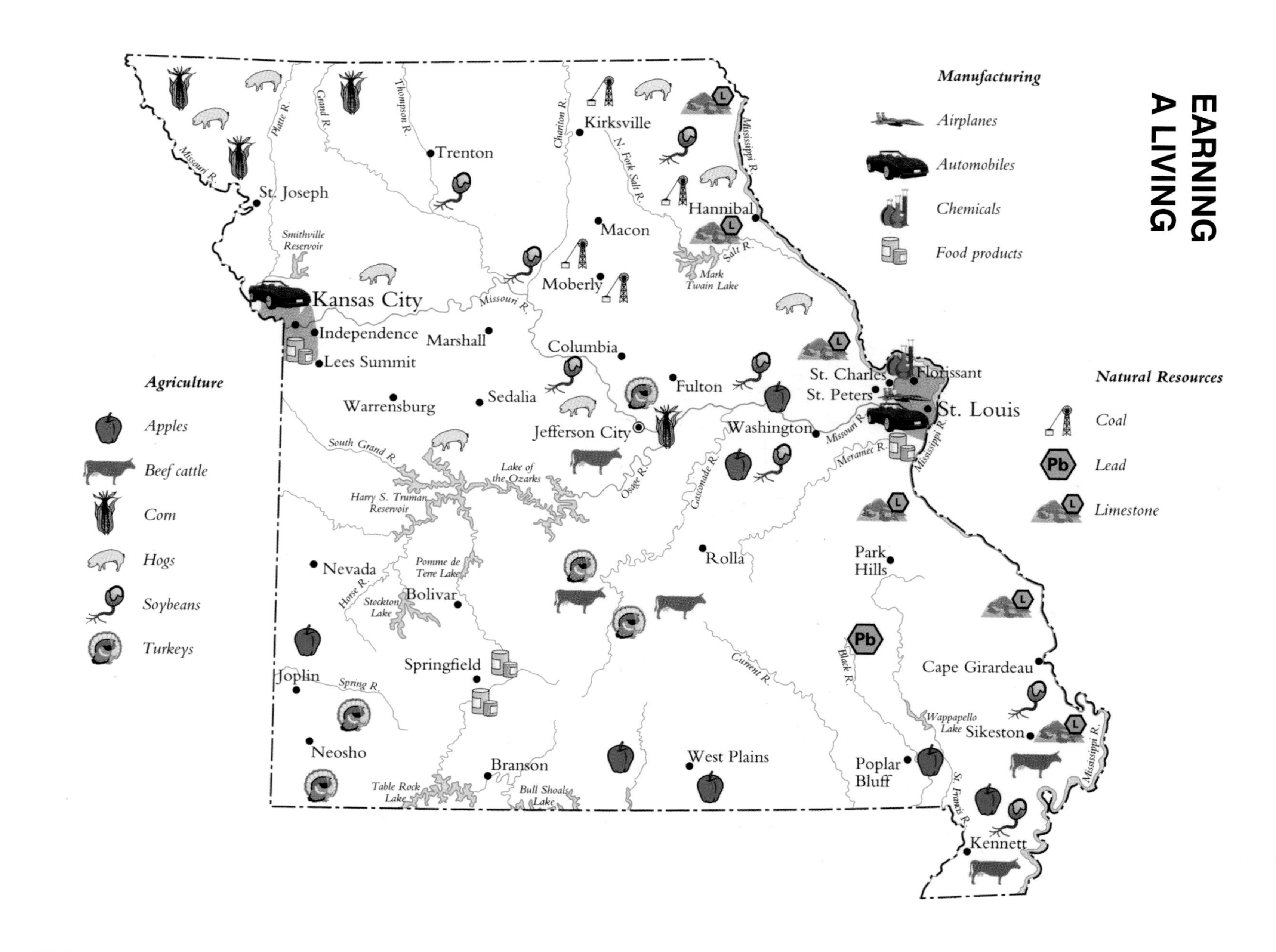

more likely to be fed to livestock. Cotton and hay are other common farm products. Cow farms are mostly located on central and southern Missouri land, whereas corn and soybeans are grown in the northern part of the state. Fruits such as apples, grapes, and watermelon are welcome treats from the state's farmers and are also sold in many other states.

AN ODOR PROBLEM WITH GIANT FARMS

Giant farms can have great environmental impacts. The sewage created by large hog farms is channeled into outdoor lagoons. It is often improperly treated or contained and sometimes leaks into the local water supply. In 1999 fifty-two enraged Missouri families won a lawsuit against the Continental Grain Company, one of the nation's largest producers of pork, for the horrible smell it produced. Described by a neighbor as "a devastating, ugly odor," the smell rises from bacteria in hog manure. Researchers are adding bacteria-killing substances to the manure to see if this will reduce the smell. Others suggest simply covering the lagoons. But "the sheer volume of manure produced by thousands of hogs is a real test for any lagoon," said Dennis Sievers, an agricultural engineer at the University of Missouri. "You can't just flush away your problems."

The problems continue, however. In 2008 more complaints were filed, and members of the Missouri legislature were determined to tighten laws, which should help to eliminate, or at least decrease, the smothering odors.

Lead, silver, and zinc are mined in Missouri.

MINERALS ROUND UP THE ECONOMIC LIST

Missouri has several minerals that are mined and sold and thus contribute to the state's economy. The most important is lead. Other common minerals in the state include copper, zinc, and silver. Limestone is cut out of deep quarries in almost every part of the state. It is estimated that about 6 billion tons of coal are yet to be mined. Small reserves of oil and gas are located along the western borders of the state. Other minerals that Missouri yields are cobalt, nickel, and tungsten.

The economic outlook for Missouri is largely dependent on the economic outlook of the nation. At the beginning of 2009 the nation was suffering from an economic recession. Many businesses, large and small, were laying off employees. Banks were failing. People were losing their homes due to bankruptcy. Missouri's economy remained strong but was not immune from those economic hardships. Hope arose that at least the service industries would remain strong and able to provide jobs. Export businesses were thriving. And the federal government was promising to help finance the state's efforts to start public works projects, such as repairing bridges and roads. No doubt, Missouri's well-rounded economy will help the state to weather the economic storm.

for fishing or canoeing. Boaters can also drift lazily down the winding Osage River as it flows between magnificent limestone bluffs crowned with groves of trees.

At Ha Ha Tonka State Park, a ruined castle looks out over the lake. At the end of the nineteenth century Kansas City millionaire Robert McClure Snyder visited the area. Because he loved its limestone bluffs and oak and hickory forests, he built his dream house there in the style of a European castle. Time has ravaged the castle—in 1942 a fire burned out the insides—but the outer walls still stand. Visitors can admire the ruins and enjoy the spectacular view of the wooded cliffs and streams.

Lake of the Ozarks, located in the heart of Missouri, is the Midwest's premier lake resort destination.

In 2007 the Butterfly Palace opened its doors in Branson. There visitors walk through a rain forest–type landscape among a thousand uncaged tropical butterflies. The Palace also offers a 3-D movie that captures the entire life cycle of a butterfly. There are a mirror maze, an insect zoo, and many reptiles to see as well.

KANSAS CITY, HERE I COME

"Who in Europe, or in America for that matter, knows that Kansas City is one of the loveliest cities on earth?" asked writer André Maurois.

Kansas City is indeed a hidden treasure. Although it is well known for its barbecue and jazz, few people realize it also has more fountains than any other city in the world except Rome, Italy. It is home to two excellent art museums and a surprising assortment of public sculpture.

Kansas City is the largest city in Missouri with a population of around 450,000 people.

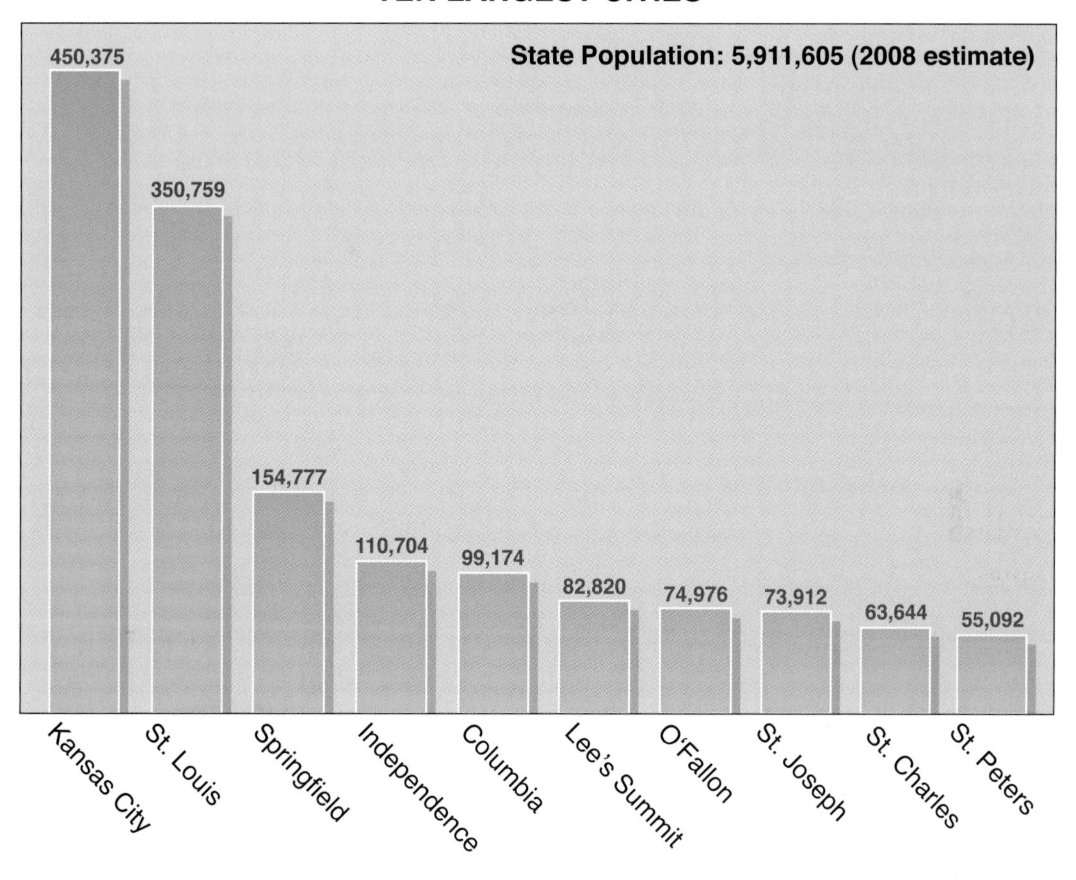

The Nelson-Atkins Museum of Art has one of the finest collections of Asian art in the world and a sculpture garden featuring a dozen works by the English artist Henry Moore, who created large, abstract representations of the human body. A visitor can see some surprising art before even entering the museum. On the spacious green lawn in front of the stately stone building, four huge red and white badminton birdies lie scattered. It looks as if some careless, gigantic

JAZZ REBORN

Kansas City is enjoying a revival. Back in the 1930s music clubs rocked and jumped with the playing of such jazz greats as Count Basie and Charlie Parker. The jazz scene has dwindled over the decades, but new life is being breathed into it today.

The jazz rebirth has included improving the city's neglected downtown area and restoring the once-famous jazz club district. The city has built the American Jazz Museum, the Gem Theater, and the Negro Leagues Baseball Museum to attract jazz lovers and tourists to the area, and they expect nightclubs and restaurants to follow.

The restoration aroused some controversy, though. Some citizens felt that money was being thrown away on a project that would not last, in a run-down part of town. And Kansas City mayor Emanuel Cleaver was criticized when he spent $140,000 of public money on a clear-plastic saxophone!

But that was a very special saxophone. It was the one Charlie Parker had played in the 1953 Massey Hall concert in Toronto, Canada—which some music lovers claim was the greatest jazz concert ever. Many Kansas Citians now feel the instrument was worth the price. That piece of jazz history has added a unique flavor to the museum. At the grand opening, actor and musician Harry Belafonte said, "There's obviously a history here that refuses to pass. It endures."

badminton players left them there after a game. When that extraordinary sculpture was first proposed, one critic objected that the museum's "majestic front lawn does not need to be cluttered with silly pop-art." Public dispute grew bitter over that artwork, but it is now a great tourist attraction and a distinctive landmark.

Another Kansas City landmark, the Kemper Museum of Contemporary Art, contains modern art, such as the paintings of Georgia O'Keefe, who made richly colored close-up views of flowers and views of the sunbaked desert near her New Mexico home. The Kemper Museum's entrance is presided over an enormous bronze spider.

At the Kemper Museum of Contemporary Art you will find works by modern and contemporary artists from around the world.

The Arabia *Steamboat Museum exhibits salvage from a sunken steamboat.*

Kansas City's museums don't contain just art. The *Arabia* Steamboat Museum is certainly worth a visit. In 1856 the steamboat *Arabia* hit a log snag while steaming up the Missouri River. It sank, bringing its 200 tons of cargo to the bottom. Flooding later caused the river to change course, and the sunken boat ended up buried in what was to become a farmer's field in Kansas. In 1989 it was dug out from under 45 feet of mud. The museum displays objects recovered from the sunken boat—the largest collection of pre–Civil War artifacts in existence. Being buried deep in mud helped to preserve much of the cargo, since the lack of oxygen prevented things from rusting and decaying. Archaeologists even dug out glass bottles of pickles, and the pickles were still bright green and tasty looking!

Another unusual museum in Kansas City is the Toy & Miniature Museum. Housed in a 1911 mansion, the rare collection boasts antique toys and small-scale replicas of houses, furniture, and objects. Many of the miniature objects are functional—scissors can actually cut, clocks can be wound, and musical instruments can be played. "I'm not interested in dolls," said one Kansas City resident, "but the Miniature Museum was great. I was surprised. Everyone I know who's been there really liked it. Even boys like it."

After all the sightseeing in Kansas City, visitors often head over to Arthur Bryant's for a delicious barbecue sandwich. They pile smoked meat onto a plate and serve it with a pickle and two slices of bread—one white, one brown. The dark brown, tangy sauce is in a squeeze bottle at the table. Squeeze some on your sandwich, and enjoy a classic Missouri taste!

THE FLAG: Broad red, white, and blue stripes cross Missouri's flag, symbolizing the state's loyalty to the Union. In the flag's center is the state seal surrounded by twenty-four stars, indicating that Missouri was the twenty-fourth state to enter the Union.

THE SEAL: In the state seal two grizzly bears representing Missourians' strength and bravery hold a shield that reads "United We Stand, Divided We Fall." Also on the shield are symbols representing the United States and Missouri.

State Survey

Statehood: August 10, 1821

Origin of Name: From the Illiniwek word *Missouri*, which means "owner of big canoes"

Nickname: Show Me State

Capital: Jefferson City

Motto: The welfare of the people shall be the supreme law

Bird: Bluebird

Flower: Hawthorn

Tree: Flowering dogwood

Insect: Honeybee

Mineral: Galena

Rock: Mozarkite

Bluebird

Hawthorn

THE MISSOURI WALTZ

President Harry S. Truman loved to play "The Missouri Waltz" on the piano in the White House. It has been recorded over the years by such performers as Bing Crosby, Guy Lombardo, Gene Autry, and Perry Como. Written in 1914 by James Royce Shannon with music by John Valentine Eppel and arranged by Frederick Knight Logan, it was adopted as the official state song in 1949.

GEOGRAPHY

Highest Point: 1,771 feet above sea level, at Taum Sauk Mountain

Lowest Point: 230 feet above sea level, along the St. Francis River near Caldwell

Area: 69,704 square miles

Greatest Distance North to South: 319 miles

Greatest Distance East to West: 365 miles

Bordering States: Iowa to the north; Illinois, Kentucky, and Tennessee to the east; Arkansas to the south; Oklahoma, Kansas, and Nebraska to the west

Hottest Recorded Temperature: 118 degrees Fahrenheit at Clinton on July 15, 1936; at Lamar on July 18, 1936; and at Union and Warsaw on July 14, 1954

Coldest Recorded Temperature: –40 °F at Warsaw on February 13, 1905

Average Annual Precipitation: 40 inches

Major Rivers: Black, Chariton, Current, Gasconade, Grand, Meramec, Mississippi, Missouri, Osage

Major Lakes: Lake of the Ozarks, Pomme de Terre, Stockton, Table Rock, Taneycomo, Harry S. Truman, Mark Twain

Trees: ash, bald cypress, cottonwood, elm, flowering dogwood, hickory, maple, oak, shortleaf pine, sweet gum

Wild Plants: aster, goldenrod, milkweed, mint, mistletoe, rose, verbena, violet

Animals: beaver, cottontail rabbit, fox, muskrat, opossum, raccoon, skunk, squirrel, white-tailed deer

Muskrat

Birds: Baltimore oriole, blue jay, bobwhite, cardinal, goldfinch, mockingbird, purple finch, whippoorwill, woodpecker

Fish: bass, bluegill, catfish, crappie, jack salmon, trout

Endangered Animals: Curtis pearlymussel, fat pocketbook, gray bat, Higgins eye mussel, Indiana bat, least tern, Ozark big-eared bat, pallid sturgeon, pink mucket, Topeka shiner

Endangered Plants: Missouri bladderpod, pondberry, running buffalo clover

TIMELINE

Missouri History

12,000–8000 CE Earliest known humans, big game hunters of mastodons and mammoths, live in what later becomes Missouri.

8000–1000 BCE Ancient people catch fish and small game, and eat wild plants. They begin to create permanent settlements in the area, including burial mounds.

500 BCE–900 CE Ancient people begin to make pottery and bows and arrows. They also plant such crops as maize.

900–1500 The Mississippian Indian culture, people with a highly complex social, political, and economic structure.

1500 The Osage, Delaware, Shawnee, and other Indians live in what is now Missouri.

1673 French explorers Jacques Marquette and Louis Joliet are likely the first Europeans to see the mouth of the Missouri River.

1682 France claims Missouri.

1735 The first permanent white settlement in Missouri is established at Sainte Genevieve.

1764 St. Louis is founded.

1774 The first school in Missouri opens.

1803 Missouri becomes a U.S. territory as part of the Louisiana Purchase.

1804 Meriwether Lewis and William Clark leave St. Louis on their mission to explore the land gained through the Louisiana Purchase.

1808 The *Missouri Gazette*, Missouri's first newspaper, begins publication in St. Louis.

1811 The second-worst earthquake ever in U.S. history strikes New Madrid.

1812 Missouri Territory is established.

1817 The *Zebulon Pike* becomes the first steamboat to travel up the Mississippi River to St. Louis.

1821 Missouri becomes the twenty-fourth state.

1825 The Osage Indians surrender the last of their lands in Missouri and move west, to Kansas.

1841 The first wagon trains to travel the Oregon Trail leave Independence.

1849 Fire destroys most of downtown St. Louis.

1851 Missouri's first railroad is built.

1854 Border wars erupt between proslavery Missourians and antislavery Kansans.

1857 The U.S. Supreme Court rules that Missourian Dred Scott must remain a slave, even though he has lived in free territories.

1860 The first Pony Express riders leave St. Joseph, Missouri, carrying mail bound for California.

1861–1865 The Civil War is fought.

1873 The nation's first public kindergarten opens in St. Louis.

1882 The notorious outlaw Jesse James is killed in St. Joseph.

1904 St. Louis hosts a world's fair.

1917–1918 More than 140,000 Missourians fight in World War I.

1931 The Osage River is dammed, creating Lake of the Ozarks.

1941 The United States enters World War II.

1945 Missourian Harry S. Truman becomes thirty-third U.S. president; the state's fourth and present constitution is adopted.

1965 The Gateway Arch monument in St. Louis is completed.

1987 Ann K. Covington becomes the first woman appointed to the Missouri Supreme Court.

1988 Richard Gephardt, U.S. congressman from Missouri, runs for president.

1992 Voters approve riverboat gambling on the ponds off the Missouri and Mississippi rivers.

1993 The Great Flood devastates parts of Missouri.

1995 Scientists and descendants gather in Kearney as Jesse James's remains are dug up.

2001 Missouri's John Ashcroft becomes U.S. attorney general.

2008 St. Louis is declared a national disaster area after record-breaking floods.

2009 Democrat Jay Nixon takes oath as Missouri's fifty-fifth governor.

ECONOMY

Agricultural Products: apples, beef cattle, chickens, corn, dairy products, hogs, peaches, sorghum, soybeans, turkeys, wheat

Manufactured Products: airplanes, automobiles, beer, cans, chemicals, food products, printed materials, railroad cars

Corn

Natural Resources: clay, coal, iron ore, lead, limestone, sand and gravel

Business and Trade: banking, insurance, real estate, telecommunications, transportation, wholesale and retail trade

CALENDAR OF CELEBRATIONS

Eagle Days Each January bird lovers flock to Clarksville to watch eagles dive and swoop and fish near 500-foot-tall bluffs along the Mississippi River. The event also features special eagle exhibits and eagle-viewing tours.

Wurstfest In March the historic town of Hermann honors a traditional German delicacy, the sausage, with a festival featuring sausage-making demonstrations and lots of tasty samples.

St. Louis Storytelling Festival Some of the best storytellers in the nation captivate listeners at this popular May event.

Lewis and Clark Rendezvous See how people lived in Missouri's early days at this May event in St. Charles. History buffs bring the lives of fur traders, American Indians, and soldiers to life, and craftspeople sell their handmade wares.

Scott Joplin Ragtime Festival Each June music lovers from all over the world descend on Sedalia to listen to lively music, trade archival sheet music, and learn more about the ragtime master.

Ozark Empire Fair The second-largest fair in Missouri, Springfield's Ozark Empire Fair in late July and early August includes livestock competitions featuring llamas, rabbits, goats, and other animals; a petting zoo; parades; and lots of amusement park rides and unusual fair food.

Lewis and Clark Rendezvous

Japanese Festival

Moonlight Ramble The world's largest nighttime bicycle event, this August extravaganza in St. Louis begins in the evening with clinics and demonstrations. But the main event doesn't start until midnight, when the bicyclists head off on a 20-mile tour.

Japanese Festival Each September the Missouri Botanical Garden in St. Louis honors Japanese culture. During the day visitors can sample traditional food, music, and crafts, and then at night stroll through the lovely Japanese Garden, where lanterns lining the paths light up the water.

Prairie Day Each September hayrides, music, and crafts demonstrations are all part of this celebration of pioneer life in Diamond.

Festival of America Each September and October Silver Dollar City hosts the nation's largest gathering of craftspeople. Visitors can see stained-glass artisans, doll makers, and glassblowers demonstrate their art; hear lots of foot-stomping music; and munch on foods from across the nation.

Deutsch Country Days Find out how Missouri's early German immigrants lived at this October event in Marthasville. Sheepshearing, wool dying, rug making, and dozens of other crafts are demonstrated.

Applefest Celebration Press your own apple cider, enjoy delicious apple dumplings or apple butter, and then wash it all down with homemade root beer. Many visitors also buy baskets of apples grown in nearby orchards at this October festival in Weston.

Festival of Lights During the winter holiday season millions of lights blaze brightly in Springfield. Hundreds of displays fill the fairgrounds, and a decorated train zips around town.

STATE STARS

Robert Altman (1925–2006) was a director famous for his innovative, irreverent films, such as *Nashville* and *The Player*, which often had lots of characters and interweaving stories. Early in his career he directed television programs, including episodes of *Alfred Hitchcock Presents* and *Bonanza*. He first gained widespread attention with his 1970 movie *M*A*S*H*, about the antics of a medical unit in the Korean War. That was soon followed by such masterpieces as *McCabe and Mrs. Miller* and *The Long Goodbye*. Altman was born in Kansas City.

Robert Altman

John Ashcroft (1942–), though born in Illinois, was raised in Springfield, Missouri. After graduating from Yale University and the University of Chicago, he began his public service career as the state's auditor in 1973. He also served as Missouri's attorney general (1976–1985) and governor (1984–1993). In 1994 Ashcroft was elected to the U.S. Senate. In 2001 President George W. Bush appointed him as the U.S. attorney general, a position he relinquished in 2004.

Josephine Baker (1906–1975) was a flamboyant dancer and singer born in St. Louis. Her career took her to New York, where she gained fame performing in nightclubs. In 1925 she performed in Paris, where she was a sensation. She is credited with introducing Europeans to many African-American dances and vocal styles. Baker remained in Paris and eventually became a widely admired French citizen.

Josephine Baker

Lawrence "Yogi" Berra

Lawrence "Yogi" Berra (1925–), one of baseball's most popular figures and greatest catchers, was born in St. Louis. Berra was an outstanding defensive player. He once went 148 games without a single error. He was also a dangerous hitter, able to power all sorts of pitches out of the park for home runs. Berra played on a record ten World Series–winning New York Yankees teams. More than anything Berra is beloved for his sense of humor and skewed sayings, such as "Baseball is 90 percent mental. The other half is physical." He was elected to the National Baseball Hall of Fame in 1972.

Chuck Berry (1926–), who grew up in St. Louis, was one of the most important figures in early rock and roll, mixing rhythm and blues and country with the new sound. His first hit, "Maybelline," scored big on the pop, rhythm and blues, and country and western charts in 1955. He also wrote such classics as "Roll Over Beethoven" and "Johnny B. Goode." Berry was a wild performer, able to dance and play guitar at the same time, a feat perfected in his famous duck walk. His combination of rhythm and blues and rock and roll had a huge influence on later performers, such as the Beatles and the Rolling Stones.

Omar Bradley (1893–1981) was a general who commanded the largest group of U.S. troops ever amassed—more than a million soldiers—for the invasion of Europe during World War II. His brilliant leadership and concern for his troops made him tremendously popular. In 1949 President Harry Truman appointed him the first chairman of the Joint Chiefs of Staff. Bradley was born in Clark.

Omar Bradley

William Wells Brown (1815–1884) was the first African American to publish a novel, the first to publish a drama, and the first to publish a travel book. Brown was born a slave in Kentucky and taken to St. Louis as a child. In 1834 he escaped to the North, where he was educated and became a popular speaker about life in the American South. In 1847 he published his first book, an autobiography titled *The Narrative of William W. Brown*. In the next eleven years he published his other landmark works.

Adolphus Busch (1839–1913), one of the nation's most successful beer makers, was born in Germany. He moved to the United States in

1857 and settled in St. Louis. In 1866 Busch entered the brewing business of his father-in-law, Eberhard Anheuser. Within a few years Busch began pasteurizing the beer so it could withstand changes in temperature and be shipped all over the country. By 1901 Anheuser-Busch was the nation's largest brewing company. Busch also developed Budweiser, the world's most popular beer.

George Washington Carver (1864–1943) was the most important African-American scientist in history. He was born and raised in the Diamond/Nosho area in southwestern Missouri. He taught farmers to revive their used-up soils by rotating crops and invented hundreds of products using peanuts, sweet potatoes, and other plants. Carver received many honors both during and after his lifetime.

Walter Cronkite (1916–) is one of the country's most trusted journalists. He first made his name as a newspaper correspondent covering World War II in Europe. In 1950 he began working for CBS and helped to develop its television news department. He served as the anchor of the *CBS Evening News* from 1962 to 1981. Cronkite was born in St. Joseph.

Walter Cronkite

Walt Disney (1901–1966) was the world's most famous animator and the creator of the vast Disney empire. He was born in Illinois, but his family moved to Missouri when he was an infant, and he grew up in Marceline and St. Louis. He began doing animation in Kansas City and in 1923 moved to Hollywood. He began producing his own cartoons and soon came up with his most famous character, Mickey Mouse. Disney's studio went on to produce such animated classics as *Snow White and the Seven Dwarfs* and *Fantasia* and, later, such live-action films as *Mary Poppins*. In 1955 Disney opened Disneyland, in California, the first of his theme parks. Walt Disney World followed in 1971, in Florida.

Walt Disney

T. S. Eliot (1888–1965) was a poet who helped reshape modern literature. Eliot grew up in St. Louis, moved to London, England in 1914, and eventually became a British citizen. In 1917 his poem "The Love Song of J. Alfred Prufrock" was published. It shook up the poetry world with its use of humor and clichés. But his real triumph was his difficult, long poem *The Waste Land*, about the corruption of life after World War I, which was filled with obscure references, sometimes in other languages. Eliot was awarded the Nobel Prize for literature, the world's greatest literary honor, in 1948.

Betty Grable (1916–1973) was one of the biggest movie stars of the 1940s. Grable was dancing and singing in movie chorus lines by age fourteen. She soon graduated to starring roles, playing energetic, good-natured characters in such lively musicals as *Moon Over Miami* and *Down Argentine Way*. She also appeared in such serious films as *I Wake Up Screaming* and *A Yank in the R.A.F.* A favorite movie beauty with U.S. servicemen in World War II, Grable was born in St. Louis.

Betty Grable

Robert Heinlein (1907–1988), a Butler native, was one of science fiction's greatest writers. An engineer, Heinlein used his scientific background to make his dozens of novels realistic reading. His books are renowned for their detailed foretelling of scientific advancements, such as the development of atomic power. Heinlein won the Hugo Award for the year's best science fiction novel a record four times, for *Stranger in a Strange Land*, *The Moon Is a Harsh Mistress*, *Starship Troopers*, and *Double Star*. He also wrote many science fiction novels for young people, including *Citizen of the Galaxy* and *Time for the Stars*.

Langston Hughes (1902–1967), a writer from Joplin, was a major figure in the Harlem Renaissance, the flowering of arts in New York's most famous African-American community in the 1920s. Hughes made literary history by using the rhythms of jazz and blues in his poems, such as "The Negro Speaks of River." By the end of his life Hughes had produced more than fifty books, including the poetry collection *Weary Blues*, the novel *Not Without Laughter*, and the short story collection *The Ways of White Folks*.

Jesse James (1847–1882), an outlaw who became a legend, was born in Clay County. During the Civil War he was part of a gang of pro–Confederate raiders who wreaked havoc on Union supporters in Kansas and Missouri. After the war he and his brother Frank, together with the Younger brothers, formed a gang of bank and train robbers. He was eventually shot dead by one of his own men, who was trying to collect the reward for his capture.

Marianne Moore

Marianne Moore (1887–1972), one of America's greatest poets, was born in St. Louis. Moore wrote carefully constructed, difficult poems, often about nature. In 1952 she was awarded the Pulitzer Prize for her book *Collected Poems*. She also edited the *Dial* literary magazine for several years, using the position to encourage young writers.

J. C. Penney (1875–1971), who was from Hamilton, founded the JC Penney Company in 1913. By his retirement in 1946, there were more than 1,600 JC Penney department stores across the nation. JC Penney remains one of America's largest retailers today.

John J. Pershing (1860–1948) commanded American forces in Europe in World War I. He is renowned for maintaining the spirit of his troops and for using an aggressive, driving style of warfare that contrasted sharply with the trench warfare that European troops had been using. After the war he was given the rank General of the Armies of the United States, the highest rank ever granted to an American army officer. Pershing was from Laclede.

Joseph Pulitzer (1847–1911), an influential newspaper publisher, was born in Hungary. In 1864 he immigrated to St. Louis, where he became a reporter and eventually a member of the Missouri House of Representatives. He purchased the *St. Louis Dispatch* and *Evening Post* in 1878 and combined the newspapers to make the *St. Louis Post-Dispatch*. He later bought the *New York World*, which became famous for its vigorous reporting and exposés. By 1887 it had the largest circulation of any newspaper in the nation. Pulitzer established the Pulitzer Prizes for excellence in journalism, literature, and music.

Joseph Pulitzer

Ginger Rogers (1911–1995), an actor and dancer, is best remembered for her graceful dancing with Fred Astaire in such classic films as *Top Hat* and *Swing Time*. She also appeared in nonmusicals including *Roxie Hart* and *The Major and the Minor*. Rogers, who often played tough, wisecracking characters, won an Academy Award for Best Actress for *Kitty Foyle*. Rogers was born in Independence.

Ginger Rogers

Casey Stengel (1889–1975), one of the greatest managers in baseball history, was born in Kansas City. After many years as an outfielder, in 1931 Stengel became the manager of the Brooklyn Dodgers. He then managed several other teams before settling in with the New York Yankees in 1949. He guided them to a World Series championship his very first year. The Yankees went on to win five World Series in a row and a total of seven with Stengel at the helm. Stengel was elected to the National Baseball Hall of Fame in 1966.

Harry S. Truman (1884–1972) was the thirty-third president of the United States. Truman was known for his forthrightness and his willingness to take responsibility for his decisions, which made him both popular and controversial. Only a few months after becoming president, Truman made the decision to drop two atomic bombs on Japan, which ended World War II. He also oversaw the beginning of the Cold War, the long-standing hostility between the former Soviet Union and the United States. Truman was born in Lamar.

Mark Twain (1835–1910), one of America's favorite writers, was born in Florida, Missouri, and grew up in Hannibal. Twain worked as a printer, steamboat pilot, and miner before settling in as a writer. He first gained attention for his story "The Celebrated Jumping Frog of Calaveras County." His fame endures for such Missouri-set novels as *The Adventures of Tom Sawyer* and *The Adventures of Huckleberry Finn*. Twain was one of the first writers to write about America in everyday language and with humor. This paved the way for later American writers to use less formal language.

Mark Twain

Tom Watson (1949–) is one of the best golfers ever. After a few shaky years, by 1977 he had established himself as the top player of the time, famed for his putting mastery. Six times he was named the Professional Golfers' Association Player of the Year. Watson was born in Kansas City.

Tom Watson

Tennessee Williams (1911–1983), a leading playwright, wrote dramas with strong southern atmospheres. Williams's plays are highly emotional and poetic and often focus on memorably eccentric characters. Some people consider *A Streetcar Named Desire*, which earned Williams the 1948 Pulitzer Prize for drama, the best American play ever. He won the Pulitzer again six years later for *Cat on a Hot Tin Roof*. Both plays were adapted into successful movies. Williams grew up in St. Louis.

Shelley Winters (1922–2006) was an actor who began her career playing sultry roles but became more famous for her blowzy, loudmouthed characters. Winters earned Best Supporting Actress Oscars for her performances in *The Diary of Anne Frank* and *A Patch of Blue*. Some of her many other famous films include *A Place in the Sun*, *Lolita*, and *The Night of the Hunter*. Winters was from St. Louis.

Shelley Winters

Gateway Arch (St. Louis) The majestic, gleaming 630-foot monument honors St. Louis's nineteenth-century role as the Gateway to the West.

City Museum (St. Louis) Walk through the mouth of a giant whale, find the hidden staircase in an old fort, or get lost in the man-made caves—you will be astonished by the exhibits at this magical museum.

City Museum

St. Louis Science Center (St. Louis) Feel the earth move in a simulated earthquake, hear a huge dinosaur roar, and climb into a cave at this museum filled with hundreds of interactive exhibits.

Missouri Botanical Garden (St. Louis) After gazing at lots of exotic flowering plants and making your way through a hedge maze, you may enjoy taking a breather in the peaceful Japanese Garden.

Missouri Botanical Garden

Museum of Transportation (St. Louis) This museum has one of the biggest collections of railroad cars in the country, along with a huge number of cars, trucks, and buses. There's even a tugboat to be explored.

St. Louis Iron Mountain & Southern Railway (Jackson) Climb aboard an old-time railroad car and then listen to the steam engine as it pulls visitors along the tracks in a trip back in time.

Johnson's Shut-Ins State Park (Piedmont) Slip and slide down natural waterslides—"shut in" between rock walls—in this park full of stunning gorges and dramatic boulders.

Elephant Rocks State Park (Graniteville) A line of huge rocks gave this park its name. After exploring the boulders, many visitors want to try their hand at fishing.

Onondaga Cave (Leasburg) Extraordinary mineral formations are the stars here, where the creatures that live underground are revealed to visitors to the cave.

Elephant Rocks State Park

Ozark National Scenic Riverways

Ozark National Scenic Riverways (Van Buren) People come from far and wide to canoe or raft down the Current and Jacks Fork rivers through dense forests and past looming bluffs.

Laura Ingalls Wilder Historic Home and Museum (Mansfield) On a visit to the house where the author of the Little House on the Prairie series spent most of her life, visitors will find lots of family pictures and possessions along with displays about pioneer times.

Glade Top Trail (Ava) The views are spectacular on this scenic byway, especially when the wildflowers are in bloom or when the leaves explode in a fall spectacle of color. It's also a great place to spy wildlife, such as wild turkeys and roadrunners.

Ha Ha Tonka State Park (Camdenton) The ruins of a magnificent castle overlooking the Lake of the Ozarks are the centerpiece of this park. Visitors can also walk along trails that pass by natural bridges, through collapsed caves, and near bubbling streams.

Hank Weinmeister's House of Butterflies (Osage Beach) Hundreds of butterflies live freely among the lush plants there, sometimes landing on flowers and sometimes on visitors' heads.

Ha Ha Tonka State Park

State Capitol

State Capitol (Jefferson City) The Thomas Hart Benton mural seen on the tour of the magnificent domed capitol is a highlight of a visit to Jefferson City.

American Jazz Museum (Kansas City) At this unique museum you can learn about jazz and some of its greatest performers, including Kansas Citian Charlie Parker. You may also experiment with recording equipment in a studio and sometimes even hear live performances.

Pony Express National Memorial

Pony Express National Memorial (St. Joseph) The stables where the Pony Express riders took off with their mailbags, bound for California, are now a museum. Exhibits enable visitors to choose the best horse for the first lap, send a telegraph message, and experience some of the sights and sounds of the long trip.

Squaw Creek National Wildlife Refuge (Mound City) Pelicans, eagles, and snow geese are just a few of the birds to be seen during a visit to this marshy spot.

FUN FACTS

Missouri has over 5,500 caves, more than any other state.

The first parachute jump ever took place outside St. Louis on March 1, 1912. Captain Albert Berry leaped from a plane flying at 1,500 feet.

The 1904 world's fair in St. Louis produced lots of tasty firsts. The world's first ice cream cone was served there, along with the first cotton candy, the first hot dog on a bun, and the first iced tea. The soft drink Dr. Pepper was also first introduced at the fair.

Find Out More

If you want to learn more about Missouri, start by checking your local library or bookstore or on the Internet for these titles.

GENERAL STATE BOOKS

Blashfield, Jean F. *Missouri* (America the Beautiful). New York: Children's Press, 2008.

Heinrichs, Ann. *Missouri.* Mankato, MN: Child's World, 2005.

Lago, Mary Ellen. *Missouri* (Welcome to the U. S. A.). New York: Children's Press, 2008.

SPECIAL INTEREST BOOKS

Brown, John W. *Missouri Legends: Famous People from the Show Me State.* St. Louis, MO: Reedy Press, 2008.

Burgan, Michael. *The Missouri Compromise.* Mankato, MN: Compass Point Books, 2006.

Satterfield, Archie. *Backroads & Byways of Missouri: Drives, Day Trips & Weekend Excursions.* Woodstock, VT: Countryman, 2008.

Strait, James. *Weird Missouri: Your Travel Guide to Missouri's Local Legends and Best Kept Secrets.* New York: Sterling, 2008.

FICTION

Jackson, Louise A. *Exiled: From Tragedy to Triumph on the Missouri Frontier.* Waco, TX: Eakin Press, 2007.

WEBSITES

Missouri Department of Natural Resources
www.dnr.mo.gov
Missouri's Department of Natural Resources offers a guide to state parks and historic sites.

Missouri State Government
www.mo.gov
At this website you will find information about Missouri's state government and history, as well as photographs of some of Missouri's best natural sites.

Missouri Tourism
www.visitmo.com
This site provides information for tourists as well as for residents about fun places to visit.

The Missourian

www.columbiamissourian.com/stories/2007/04/14/ancient-history/

The online magazine *Missourian* offers information about the ancient history of the state.

State Kids Page

www.sos.mo.gov/kids/

The Missouri secretary of state's page for kids brings together a lot of interesting facts about the state and its government.

Index

Page numbers in **boldface** are illustrations and charts.

ABOUT THE AUTHORS

Michelle Bennett is a writer living in New York City. In her travels throughout Missouri she roamed its countryside, savored its food, and enjoyed talking to its people. The Show Me State is permanently on Bennett's go-back-to-often list.

Joyce Hart has written more than thirty books and enjoys leisurely car trips across the United States. She has driven past the St. Louis Loop and across the Missouri River as she meandered through the Midwest. She writes books during the rainy winter months in her cabin on the Hood Canal in Washington. In the summer she hits the road again with her dog, Molly, exploring the backroads of different states.